Mrs. Peale and I saw [...] absolutely wonderf[...] on the large audien[...] impression on us. Y[...] and comes through with compelling power.

Dr. Norman Vincent Peale
Author
The Power of Positive Thinking

CONQUERING LIFE'S OBSTACLES is not just another motivational book. It is a work book with specific game plans on How To Do It. A real guide book to achievement.

Rich DeVos
President
Amway Corporation

Gerry Robert lives the Possibility Thinker's life. He is living proof that tough times never last but tough people do. This book successfully marries life changing wisdom and inspiration from the heart, born out of experience.

Dr. Robert Schuller
Pastor
The Crystal Cathedral

I have a high regard for Gerry Robert and the things he has achieved. By the time you have finished this book, so will you. But more importantly, you will have at your disposal relevant and reliable tools to deal with your own obstacles.

Kenneth Blanchard, Ph.D.
Co-author
The One Minute Manager

DEDICATION

TO MY LATE FATHER AND BROTHER,
WHOM I LOVED SO MUCH AND
MISS YET TODAY:
"I'M MAKING IT!
I'M TAKING CARE OF MYSELF!"

CONQUERING Life's Obstacles

Gerry Robert

PPC
Books

Copyright © 1990 by Gerry E. Robert

Canadian Cataloguing in Publication Data

Robert, Gerry, 1958-
    Conquering life's obstacles

ISBN   1-895250-00-5

1. Success.   2. Success in business.   I. Title.

BF 637.S8R6   1990   158'.1   C90-094513-3

Software supplied and supported by :

Beaumont International
375 Bay Mills Blvd.
Suite 407
Agincourt, Ontario
M1T 2G6
TEL: (416) 754-2432

Printed in Canada
Second Printing 1991

CONTENTS

ACKNOWLEDGEMENTS

To begin, I must thank my best friend and wife Anne. She loved me and supported my passion to help others enough to allow me the time to think and create. Her sacrifice and input were essential to the writing of this book.

Secondly, my creative juices flowed and did so according to schedule because of the combined effort of my Attila The Hun Committee. This small group of advisers have done more for me than they will ever know. In addition to watching for deadlines, content development, focus and quality in my writing, they demonstrated in practical terms what commitment is all about. Peter Lees, Jennifer Mason and Ron Purcell are three of the most dedicated, honest and caring people I know.

I am also grateful for the tireless editing of Cathy Montgomery, who's work was temporarily interrupted to give birth to a beautiful daughter, Sara, but resumed promptly between feedings.

Thirdly, I must acknowledge the people who have had an impact on my life. I am forever indebted to the people who showed me how and gave me the strength to conquer my own obstacles. They include Norman & Jim Sharkey, Robert Marwick, and Bill & Marion Forrester. For their support over the years I need to thank Scott and Pam Campbell, Robert and Jane Brglez, Jean and Bill Gardner, Paul and Linda Carter, Garry and Rebbeca Targett. And my mother and family who's strength in the face of difficult times have kept me going.

Finally, to my son Corey - who is still too young to understand just how he fills our lives with joy and provides both Anne and I with more than enough reason to <u>CONQUER LIFE'S OBSTACLES.</u>

INTRODUCTION

I was sitting in my apartment, when, all of a sudden, the front door came flying off the hinges. I heard the sound of breaking glass and cracking wood. Over a dozen police officers came running toward me with revolvers drawn. They crushed me against the wall and put a gun in my ear and said, "If you move one muscle, we'll blow your head off". I believed them.

That happened over a decade ago. It was my darkest moment. It was the most frightening experience of my life. It surely was the most difficult. In one sense, what happened that day was the most negative event I have ever been through, but in another, it was definitely the most positive.

Something happens when you look down the barrel of a .38 pistol and you are convinced that at any moment your life may end. Something sure happened to me.

That one event is responsible for my leaving a life of violent crime and embarking on the greatest trip of discovery and self-development, a trip which has allowed me to impact the lives of thousands. Through television appearances, radio interviews, seminars and corporate speaking engagements, I share the story of how I conquered the success blockers which prevented me from developing my full potential and enjoying life.

I grew up in a home with a father who suffered from alcoholism. We lived in "the project", a fancy name for a low - rental development, rampant with crime, drugs and violence.

At ten years of age, adults encouraged me to steal. I didn't let them down. I enjoyed the attention. In the years that followed things grew worse, considerably worse. At thirteen, a friend showed me some white pills he had bought with money from a stolen purse. They made me forget the pain. During the "trip" I didn't think about what was happening. I could escape for a while. I fell in love with "intoxication". I was in that condition as frequently and as intensely as I could be, even at that young age.

I was drinking in bars and was kicked out of school at fifteen. I started working full-time just before my sixteenth birthday. I had my first run-in with the police that year. I was arrested and convicted for grand theft auto.

By the time I was eighteen, I had committed many crimes including shoplifting, kidnapping, drug trafficking, abduction and armed robbery.

In February, 1977, I was arrested for armed robbery. On September 6, 1977, my life was turned around forever. It is a day I will never forget! On that day, I left the life of crime and deceit. I got off the road of failure and got on the road of success. I left negative thinking behind and chose positive thinking instead. On that very special day, I began to change from a life of destruction, despair and poverty to enjoy a life of value, happiness and prosperity.

Shortly before that September date, a physician certified that I was an alcoholic and a drug addict and he recommended I move into Our House Recovery Home, which I did. What I saw in that recovery home through its residents made me want to change. And change I did!

I became enthused about life. For the first time ever, I sensed I could do something with my life. I had not known very many people who were not alcoholics or drug addicts. Most everyone I knew was heavily into crime. Almost everyone I knew was unhappy. The people in this recovery home were different and I wanted to be like them.

That was over a decade ago. Since that day, I have never touched one drop of booze, drugs or committed another crime. I conquered my success-blockers, not alone, not without help and not without a tremendous amount of hard work, the hardest I have ever experienced. But I did it! If I could do it, imagine what you could accomplish.

Just think for a moment of the people you know and you'll realize that most of them live within negative parameters. They "can't", they "won't", they "don't", their life is a cycle of criticism and complaint. And yet it is possible for each of us to control our destiny provided we remove the SUCCESS-BLOCKERS, which we all face. A SUCCESS-BLOCKER is a barrier or obstacle. It is whatever comes between you and your goals or dreams. These dreams and goals will be realized when you remove the:

MOTIVATIONAL SUCCESS-BLOCKERS

DIRECTIONAL SUCCESS-BLOCKERS

OPERATIONAL SUCCESS-BLOCKERS

RELATIONAL SUCCESS-BLOCKERS

Many people are like the art student touring a great gallery in Florence, Italy. He made critical remarks about every masterpiece he saw. The guide was getting more upset by the minute. Finally, he just couldn't take it any longer. He walked up to the student and said, "Young man, these masterpieces are not on trial---you are!"

Life can be tough, can't it? It is sometimes hard and cruel. I have found that no matter who a person is or what they have achieved, everyone faces problems. It is how we view and respond to problems that determines what we will become in life. My challenge to you is: find ways to put your problems in perspective.

When Faced With Problems - The Choice Is Yours

You Can...   ### Instead Of...

You Can...	Instead Of...
● Focus on Solutions	Problems
● Choose Growth	Despairing
● Become Better	Becoming Bitter
● See The Diamond	Disaster
● Be Solution-Orientated	Problem-Orientated
● Have Faith	Having Fear
● Seek The Best	Seeking The Worst
● Help	Hindering
● Enjoy Life Now	Waiting For "Someday"
● Assume Responsibility	Assigning Blame
● Generate Ideas	Giving Up

On the following pages I hope to help you develop the personal power you need to achieve your dreams and see your goals come to reality. The material has been tested and proven in the labs of the University of Hard Knocks.

This book is about taking charge of your life and moving toward a deeper sense of achievement. Who among us does not slide into ruts? A rut is nothing more than a grave with the ends kicked out. What you will gain from these pages is an awareness of the tools to protect against the SUCCESS-BLOCKERS.

Experience with me the joy of being free, the joy of self-mastery and personal power. A warning here is essential. This book isn't for cowards! Certain portions of this book may be painful.

I write about real life people and real life pain. At times that is not a pleasant thing to digest. I attempt at every turn to provide practical, easy-to-use methods, tips and techniques for us to grow by. My desire is to impact you and impact our world.

Someone once said that a "coward" is nothing more than a "tower of Jello". I'm not sure about that. I tend to agree more with the person who said a "coward" is nothing more than a "hero in need of a push".

That may just be what this book will do for you: give you that little "push", so you can develop more and more, little by little, day by day into the beautiful "hero" that you are.

Gerry   Robert
Toronto, 1990

---◆---

CONQUERING
THE
MOTIVATIONAL
SUCCESS-BLOCKERS

---◆---

CHAPTER 1

HOW TO HAVE AN ACHIEVER'S ATTITUDE ALWAYS

Have you ever wondered how some people just seem to be highly motivated most of the time? Why are they so positive even in the face of disappointments and frustrations? Why do some people wake up in the morning and say "Good morning, Lord", while others wake up and say, "Good Lord, it's morning"?

What can be done to keep your circumstances from affecting your attitude? Is it possible to stay motivated? What do those "positive thinkers" actually do to stay that way? I can answer some of these questions because I was able to live in a maximum security prison and still remain motivated. Let me illustrate some of the techniques I used.

During my seminars, I approach someone and conduct an exercise to illustrate how attitudes are formed. I tell them that they are the most incompetent person I have ever met and I then ask the audience to raise their hands if they think the person's self-esteem will suffer because of what I just did. Almost always, the majority of the crowd raise their hands, indicating that they feel that this person's attitude would be affected by what I said to him.

The answer to the question, however, is NO. A person's self-esteem would not increase or decrease based on what I said but rather by what they say to themselves about what I said.

Achiever's Attitude Formula
$$E + BS(r) = O$$

In this formula, the "E" stands for Events or Experiences. The "BS" represents Belief Systems and "(r)" Response. The "O" is Outcome. We all have Events and Experiences in life. Being called incompetent by a speaker is one example of an Experience. Our Belief Systems - what we believe about ourselves, others, and events - govern our Response. It is the "BS(r) which determines the "O" Outcomes; a high or low self-esteem in this example.

Look at it this way; If I call someone in my seminar incompetent, that is an "E", event. That person will respond to that event based on their "BS(r)", (Belief System and Response). If that person has a poor self-image and says to himself, "I am incompetent, how did he figure that out so quickly?", what would happen to his self-esteem? It would suffer, of course. He would have a negative "O" Outcome from that "E" Experience.

Imagine what would happen if instead the same person said to himself: "Now there is an interesting speaker. Out of all the people in this room, he somehow knows I can take this type of kidding. He sees that I am confident enough to be the example in this exercise. Out of everyone in the room, he picked me. HE PICKED ME!"

What impact would that type of self-talk have on this person's self-esteem? Obviously, it would get stronger. He would have a positive "O" Outcome based on his "BS(r)" Belief System Response and not on the "E" Experience.

So we see that the same experience can have either a positive or negative outcome. The key is what we say to ourselves about those events.

Take the case of the two young brothers from Texas. A mother was distraught because her two little boys were behaving badly, traumatizing their neighbourhood. One day the mother went next door and began pouring her problems out to the neighbour over coffee. The neighbour offered a solution. She explained that when she had similar difficulties with her son, she took him to confession at the local church, after which, his behaviour improved. The distraught mother decided to do the same thing for her two mischievous sons. The stern priest took the first boy into the booth and said, "Johnny, where is God?" The young boy was petrified, but said nothing. The priest repeated the question. The boy jumped from his seat, ran from the priest and motioned for his brother to run out with him. On the way out he said to his brother, "We're in big trouble now. They have lost God and they're trying to pin it on us."

Far too often in life, we want to blame the "E's" Events and Experiences for negative or undesirable "O" Outcomes. Often we can't change the events of life. Sometimes loved ones can hurt us. At times, clients will choose a competitor, the economy will fluctuate, your prices might be higher than others, your teenager will get into trouble. It's not the "E's" (Events) of life which cause poor attitudes or low motivation, but what you believe and your response to them. What you say to yourself about these things has more to do with negative outcomes than anything else.

How To Get Control Of Your Attitude

1. Control The Self-talk.

How do you react when faced with difficulties? In 1988, my wife Anne began to slur her words, dropping things, and her coordination was off. She could not raise her eyes above mid-range, and her balance was impaired. If she tried to walk toe to heel she would literally fall over.

The doctor said she had a virus and admitted her to hospital for further observation. I figured they would prescribe medication and everything would be back to normal, but we were informed that this virus attached itself to the base of the brain, and it was eating away at the nerve endings. It was a rare illness called Gillian Barre Syndrome.

The doctor said she would probably get a lot worse before she got better. This illness usually lasts several months.

It often affects the muscles which control breathing. My wife would probably need life support systems to keep her alive. In these situations it is so easy to loose control of our thinking. Instead, we decided to live one day at a time, rely on our friends, family and faith to see us through. We did not loose control of our rational minds. We refused to dwell on the "What would happen if..." questions. We hung onto hope. It worked! Anne eventually recovered and is fine today.

People with my background are not well-known for their love for and use of poetic literature, but one poem helps illustrate a point I try to make at almost every speech I give. It is called "The Man In The Glass". One particular verse, the last, brings home a very important message,

"You can fool the whole world down the pathway of life

And get pats on your back as you pass

But your final reward will be heartaches and tears

If you cheat the man in the glass."

One of the ways we cheat the person in the glass is by what we say to the person looking back. We often hurt ourselves by repeating lies about who we are, our limitations and dwelling on our weaknesses. A saleswoman found she sold more of a cosmetic cream when she stopped telling her customers it would "restore" their complexion and began saying it would "preserve" their complexion. What you say to yourself will yield good, healthy results if you say the right things.

Reverend Scott Campbell uses the following exercise to make a similar point. Put your thumb up in front of your eyes. Now focus in on your thumb nail. Leave your thumb where it is but now focus in on another object in the room. What happens? How many thumbs do you see? Is the thumb in focus? NO! It is impossible to focus on two objects at the same time. The same can be said for positive and negative statements about ourselves. We will either focus in on the constructive or the destructive side.

Do you ever hear yourself say things like:

No one likes me

I have nothing to contribute

I am ugly

If only...

I am terrible at that

Nothing good ever happens to me

I'm really unlucky

Life is really tough

I am dumb

I don't count

My opinion doesn't matter

I'm worthless

I'm not important

I'm really scared

I can't

I could never do that

I'm no good

Any time you hear negative self talk, STOP IT! You are in control. You have the ability to confront your feelings. Exercise command of what you say to yourself. A great preacher friend of mine, Howard Hunt says, "You are not what you think you are - what you think - You are!"

2. Be Aware of Your Limiting Belief Systems.

Positive thinkers, people who are highly motivated and optimistic, live their lives by a certain belief system. Many adopt a motto or creed similar to the one introduced by Dr. Robert Schuller, author of <u>Move Ahead with Possibility Thinking</u>.

He calls it the Possibility Thinker's Creed and it goes like this:

"When faced with a mountain
I WILL NOT QUIT!
I will keep on striving until I climb over
Find a pass through
Tunnel underneath
or simply stay and turn the mountain into a gold mine
With God's help - **I WILL NOT QUIT**"

Now that's a powerful belief system! Those verses have made dramatic changes in my life. When tempted to pack it in, I would remember that creed and it helped me to change my belief system about problems.

REJECT ABSOLUTE ASSOCIATIONS

Without our being aware of it, we hold to absolutes which are false. It was an absolute that in prison you never say you will never be back. I rejected that absolute and have never been back, and never will. I rejected the absolute association between being in prison and not being happy. I was happy in prison. I had decided to become a better person while I was in there. I read dozens of self-help books. I attended meetings that helped me change. I rejected the notion that prison could not be productive. I left that place a much different person than when I entered.

CHANGE YOUR FOCUS!

THIS	DOESN'T ALWAYS MEAN...	INSTEAD ASK...
Unfaithfulness	Your marriage is over.	Where can we get help?
A terrible economy	You can't make money in sales.	Who could give me referrals?
Marriage is stale	I don't love him.	What is there to love about this person?
Being Overweight	You can't lose weight.	What one thing can I do to lose weight?
Your boss is a jerk	You can't be happy at work.	How can we get along?

Belief Systems

Read through this list. Using the following scale, rate yourself. Which one or two areas tend to be major struggling points?

U = Usually S = Sometimes R = Rarely

___I fear change
___I fear rejection
___I am critical of self
___I am easily discouraged
___I am preoccupied with past
___I am defensive
___I talk negatively of self
___I lack decisiveness
___I am critical of others
___I tend to question self
___I compare self with others
___I fear failure
___I am always pessimistic
___I feel inadequate
___I have difficulty establishing relationships
___I control others to make self look good
___I feel self-conscious
___I worry about what others think
___I need continual approval
___I am insecure around others
___I take things personally

Do you detect any areas which may be responsible for a limiting belief system? Identify the two most pronounced items and begin working on those first.

Laziness is not on this list and perhaps it should be. Laziness can ruin your attitude, unless you are like the old farmer who was sitting on his porch when asked, "How's things?" "Tolerable", came the reply. He continued, "Two weeks ago a cyclone came along and knocked down all the trees I had to chop down for this winters firewood. Then last week lightening struck the brush I had to burn to clear the fields for planting." The stranger responded, "That's remarkable, what are you doing now?" the farmer answered, "waiting for an earthquake to come along and shake the potatoes out of the ground."

At one point in my life, I would have answered "Usually" to almost everyone of those questions above. However, I have learned how harmful limiting beliefs are to my success. Today, I am enjoying a level of success and happiness I never dreamed possible, all because I became aware of the weak links in my belief system and was willing to take some risks in those areas and grow.

3. Reprogram Any Negative Mental Tapes.

Reprogramming negative mental tapes is one method of changing your perspective. Change your perspective and you change your attitude. This point is brought home in the following letter from a college student to her parents:

"Dear Mom and Dad

I wanted to let you know that I think I'm in love. I met a wonderful man. His name is Chuck, he drives a Harley Davidson motorcycle. He quit school when he was sixteen but has a good job now at K-mart. He was married at nineteen but the divorce just came through. He has three lovely kids.

I really love him and we plan to be married in the fall. I have moved into his apartment. I've quit school to help pay some of the bills. Talk to you soon. Love, your daughter.

P.S. I think I'm pregnant!"

On the next page the shocked parents read this:

"Dear Mom and Dad

Nothing I have written so far is true, it's all false. But it is true that I flunked math, got a C in English and need more money!!! I just wanted you to get that news in proper perspective."

One of the top professionals in the world of public speakers and writers is Joel Weldon. Joel is a master motivational speaker. He is well known for his saying that "Success comes in cans, not cannots".

He also shares a fantastic poem called "Build A Better You":

"Your task: to build a better world, God said.
I answered, 'How?'
The world is such a large place, so complicated now;
And I so small and useless am, there's nothing I can do."
But God in all His wisdom said,
'Just build a better You.'"

Isn't it funny when a manager builds a better manager, the whole office seems to get better. When dad builds a better dad the family seems to pull together. Isn't it true when we focus in on how we can be better, others just get better too?

Once you decide to assume responsibility for the "O's" Outcomes of your life, and have discovered any limiting beliefs about yourself, you are ready to erase the negative tapes you play inside your mind. Society, family, friends, economists, school, and sometimes even religion have programmed you to think a whole lot less about yourself than you should. The process of clearing and reprogramming those mental tapes is not easy.

I was raised in a poor neighbourhood, with an alcoholic father. Everyone I knew was on drugs or booze and in trouble with the law. Virtues such as honesty, hard work, education and positive thinking were nowhere to be found on my street. Instead, I was programmed with things like: "give-up", "think small", "you're dumb", "you'll never amount to much". I know the process of change is never easy, particularly if you have had years of negative programming, but if I could do it, so can you!

POWER STATEMENTS

"I AM A WORTHWHILE PERSON, NO MATTER WHAT YOU THINK, SAY OR DO TO ME."

One way to reprogram the negative mental tapes, is to listen to and read positive and inspirational material. Don't listen to the Rolling Stones in your car; plug in a tape from the famous motivational teacher Zig Ziglar. Forget about reading the gloomy forecasts in the newspaper; instead pick up any book by Dr. Norman Vincent Peale , Dr. Robert Schuller or Og Mandino.

If you want to get rid of "stinkin' thinkin'" search out motivators, speakers and authors. Some examples are Cavett Robert, who for years has been teaching on celebrating life; Harold Taylor, the top man on Time and Personal Management, and Rosita Perez who helps us believe in ourselves and gives us tools to become more effective in our personal and business lives.

Another way to radically alter your belief system is to get in the habit of using POWER STATEMENTS. On 3 X 5 cards, write statements of affirmation and repeat them out loud dozens of times a day. If you were to look in my car when I'm stuck in traffic, chances are you would see me holding one of my statement cards and repeating it to myself. You might think I was nuts but I know these things work. If I tell myself five thousand times, "I CAN", the next time I hear "I can't", it will be drowned out by a sea of "I CAN'S". Success comes in "CANS."

EXAMPLES OF POWER STATEMENTS

I AM LOVABLE AND CAPABLE

I AM CONFIDENT

I AM ENTHUSIASTIC

I AM A SUCCESS

I TAKE RISKS

I WILL NOT QUIT

I AM A WINNER

I LOVE MYSELF

PEOPLE LOVE ME

You can have an Achiever's Attitude Always. Easy? No! Possible, regardless of circumstances, experiences and events? Yes! Remove the MOTIVATIONAL SUCCESS-BLOCKERS by practising these steps to positive living. Watch what you say to yourself, find any weak links in your belief system, erase any negative mental tapes with the use of affirmations and power statements.

We will delve further into this subject in the next chapter as we examine the area of self-esteem. What are the causes and results of a poor sense of self-worth? How can we remove MOTIVATIONAL SUCCESS-BLOCKERS by improving how we feel about ourselves?

One lady in my SELF-ESTEEM AND PERSONAL POWER seminar said she came to improve her self-esteem because she didn't have ANY!!! I want to share with you what I told her about how she could feel better about herself.

CHAPTER 2

DEVELOP AN "I MATTER" SELF-ESTEEM

I MATTER - What's wrong with believing we are worthwhile? Isn't there a sense in which we all want to know that we count? Do we not all at times long to be deeply satisfied on the inside about ourselves. Who among us doesn't strive towards what I call the "Dignity Quest", the search for personal meaning and dignity.

I strongly suspect that self-esteem, the sense of individual worth and self-love or appreciation is a fundamental need of man. More than any other thing, we want the conscious awareness and experience of worthiness. It is the strongest, most powerful drive man has ever known - the desire and drive to matter. Every other drive attempts to satisfy that basic essential need.

The quest for love, power, pleasure, sex, status are nothing more than expressions of the primal desire to matter. They are the false symbols of significance. You might think that a certain fellow is a real clown because of his jokes. But it could be his intense hatred for self which causes him to avoid real communication. If he did look at himself he might not like what he saw, so he acts the buffoon to avoid internal pain. While trying to convince you he is something special, he is also trying to convince himself. Could the pursuit of pleasure be a disguise for an escape from self?

A young girl gives in to her boyfriend and "goes all the way" because she is afraid to lose him or be thought of as a prude. Is that the real reason? Is she afraid of rejection by her boyfriend? "Perhaps if he rejects me - everyone will reject me! I need to matter - rejection equals - you don't matter". So she does whatever she must to feel needed, wanted, worthy.

We live in a society that has mixed up the signals, misread the needs and assumed that it can satisfy the deepest longing of man. The housewife assumes that if she has the luxury of nice things she will matter. The CEO assumes that he will fill the void now that he has arrived.

What we want more than anything - more than thrills, power, money, fame, status is - to matter.

DESCRIPTION OF SELF-WORTH

This...	Instead of	This...
Poised		Tense
Confident		Confused
Bold		Timid
Enthusiastic		Bored
Successful		Failing
Energetic		Fatigued
Agreeable		Cantankerous
Positive		Negative
Self-forgiving		Self-condemning
Self respecting		Self-disgusting

INDICATORS OF AN INADEQUATE SELF-ESTEEM

Do any of these describe you? These indicators may help you understand the origins of damaging thinking.

1. You come from a dysfunctional family with apparent abandonment which might have included abuse.

2. Fear is very pronounced.

3. You give up easily! If you try too hard and fail, you may be rejected. You don't feel confident. You're scared to fail!

4. Decision-making is extremely painful.

5. You always need to be "right", "to win", "to make it".

6. You are a driven person - outwardly achieving, inwardly doubting.

7. You are overly critical of others.

8. You are driven towards perfectionism.

9. You are overly critical of yourself even publicly. Very self-conscious with poor assessment of your abilities.

10. You escape - compulsivity, booze, drugs, other addictions, fantasy, pleasure.

MEASURING HOW MUCH YOU MATTER
SELF-ESTEEM INVENTORY

In order to obtain an indication of your prevailing Self-Esteem, score the following statements as follows:

"O" If not true
"1" If somewhat true
"2" If largely true
"3" If true

L   R

1. I judge my self-worth by comparison with others.
2. I am free to speak up for my own viewpoint.
3. I am a people pleaser.
4. I rarely feel uncomfortable, and lonely when alone.
5. I am prone to condemn others.
6. I usually anticipate challenges with quiet confidence.
7. I am fearful of exposing the real me.
8. I rarely experience jealousy, envy or suspicion.
9. I am easily embarrassed by the actions of others.
10. I am appreciative of others' achievements and ideas.
11. I tend to belittle my own achievements.
12. I am not prejudiced.
13. I often blame others for my problems and mistakes.
14. I am not bothered at all by shame, guilt and remorse.
15. I habitually condemn myself for my shortcomings.
16. I am free to express love, anger, resentment and joy.
17. I frequently brag about myself.
18. I accept my own authority and do as I, myself, see fit.
19. I have an intense need for confirmation.
20. I am free to think for myself.
21. I have a strong need for recognition, and approval.
22. I normally feel good toward myself.
23. I feel weak often.
24. I am eagerly open to different ways of doing things.
25. I am a compulsive "perfectionist".
26. I normally make my own decisions.

L	R

_____ 27. I habitually deny, justify or rationalize my mistakes.

_____ 28. I have great enjoyment and zest for living.

_____ 29. I often feel inadequate to handle new situations.

_____ 30. I am usually free of inner conflict and frustration.

_____ 31. I have a driving need to prove that I matter.

_____ 32. I accept compliments without embarrassment.

_____ 33. Losing normally causes me to feel resentful.

_____ 34. I usually feel friendly toward others.

_____ 35. I am very often critical and belittling of others.

_____ 36. I am normally friendly, considerate and generous.

_____ 37. I am often compulsive about eating, or drinking.

_____ 38. I can let others be "wrong" without correcting them.

_____ 39. I experience a strong need to defend my opinions.

_____ 40. I take disagreement without feeling rejected.

_____ 41. I am very concerned about what others think of me.

_____ 42. I readily admit my mistakes, and failures.

_____ 43. I often shun new endeavors because of fear of failure.

_____ 44. I make and keep friends without trying very hard.

_____ 45. I exaggerate and lie to save face.

_____ 46. I am usually comfortable meeting new people.

_____ 47. I usually feel inferior to others.

_____ 48. I am free to give precedence to my own desires.

_____ 49. I often defer to others on account of their prestige.

_____ 50. I willingly accept responsibility for my actions.

Scoring

TOTAL OF LEFT COLUMN: _____

SUBTRACT TOTAL OF RIGHT COLUMN: – _____

EQUALS SELF-ESTEEM INDICATOR :   _____

This net score is your current Self-Esteem Indicator, or SEI. The possible range of one's Self-Esteem Indicator is from -75 (low self-esteem) to + 75 (high). Yours will fall somewhere in between. Do not be overly concerned about your SEI, even if it is negative. It can always be improved.

Remember your self-esteem indicator simply is what it IS, the automatic product of your heritage and total life experience; and thus nothing to be ashamed or embarrassed about. It is important, however, that you be honest with yourself in order to obtain as valid a score as possible, for this score is a beginning reference point in gauging your progress in building self-esteem. Also remember, that no matter how low your present SEI may be, you can bring it up to any desired level by conscientious effort.

WHAT IS AN "I MATTER" SELF-ESTEEM?

IT IS...

believing you are a masterpiece - created for greatness,

letting go of your past,

putting failure into perspective,

being proud of who you are ,

choosing the right value system,

living by the "Diamond Principle".

1. AN "I MATTER" SELF-ESTEEM MEANS...
YOU BELIEVE YOU ARE A MASTERPIECE - CREATED FOR GREATNESS!

You ARE great! You weren't put here to fail. You were not designed to lose. Defeat is not part of any masterplan! You are framed for success. You are wired to shine.

I know people, as I'm sure you do, who just sit and wait and complain and wait and complain and wait and complain about how terrible life is to them and how they will never amount to anything. "Nothing worthwhile ever happens to worthless people."

I refuse to be like that! I assume responsibility for my life and resist the masses who choose to live with mediocrity. I am created for success and I refuse the notion that I cannot make it!

An "I matter" self-esteem says "I refuse to accept anything but the masterpiece I was created to be. I matter enough to work hard to develop into that full colour work of art that I am."

Understanding that I have the seeds of success within allows me to:

- be filled with passion and enthusiasm
- control my feelings of inadequacy
- put my problems in perspective
- think creatively about solutions
- be honest even if it is painful
- risk failing
- ask for help
- think big
- conquer the Success-Blockers
- climb the mountains when I'm tired and close to giving up
- go that extra mile
- stretch myself just a little more
- refuse defeat
- remove such words as impossible from my vocabulary
- have hope no matter what.

2. AN "I MATTER" SELF-ESTEEM MEANS...
LETTING GO OF YOUR PAST

What effect does our past have on our self-esteem? One major reason so may people suffer with a poor self-esteem is because of the scars inflicted upon them from their past.

I once tried to help a pretty young woman who felt terribly ugly, dumb and dirty. When we tried to understand, we discovered that her father, a care-taker in a public grade school, had been abusing her since her childhood.

The graphic details she shared, far too sickening to ever

detail here, nauseated me but at the same time did not surprise me. Along with all the physical and sexual abuse came the scars of mental and emotional abuse.

This poor girl married at a young age to get away from the monster her siblings called "Dad". He told her all her life that if she told anyone of their secrets they would think she was crazy and not believe her. After having a baby and less than 2 years of marriage she could no longer conceal the horrendous pain of her past. The night she broke down and told her husband about the abuse was the night she found herself out on the street - totally rejected again. Her marriage ended that night.

The last thing I would ever try to suggest here is that there are simple solutions to such devastating pasts. But I will say that without putting her past in perspective she is doomed to live in it and continue to experience an "I'm worthless" self-esteem!

I doubt if any of us are not affected one way or another by our pasts. How many of us are free from its effect? How many of our perceptions about ourselves are really distortions of who we are carried on from past conditioning?

Walk by one of those curved mirrors at a country fair. You will see a distorted image of yourself. We have all seen reflections from different sources. Our parents were our mirrors when we were children. They mirrored to us either a sense of our significance as individuals or lack of value due to poor performance. We lived our lives from those mirrors. If the mirror which allows me to see myself, says "I'm not smart enough" or "I'm not good enough" then that's what I see.

People in any 12 step program such as Alcoholics Anonymous recover by dealing with their past head on. They encourage people to do a "searching and fearless moral inventory" and even to share it with another human being. They list the events of their past and omit nothing.

The self-esteem killer - GUILT!

Guilt says - "Don't get too close to people, they may find out who you really are. They may judge you. Don't express yourself." So you recoil from others because of this fear that the "real you" will come out. The fear of humiliation. Put your past in perspective, free yourself of it's clutches. Everyone is human. Not one of us is perfect. What do you have to feel guilty about?

Many of us feel guilty about something. Sir Arthur Conan Doyle decided to play a practical joke on 12 of his friends. He sent them each a telegram which read "Flee at once...all is discovered." Within 24 hours all 12 had left the country. We feel guilt for things we haven't done and things we have.

In 1924, Liberty magazine sent out 100 letters to people selected at random throughout the United States, enclosing a $1.00 bill. This is equivalent to $100.00 of today's money. The letter said it was an adjustment of an error which the addressed had complained of... which they had never done. Of the 100 recipients, 27 returned the dollar saying it was a mistake. Then in 1971, Liberty again conducted the same test. This time only 13 returned the money. Honesty is waning.

Perhaps a talk with a person acquainted with the great guilt-buster - "The man upstairs" would be in order? I became free from guilt and enjoyed a clean slate when I decided to confess my past and seek forgiveness, both from people and my creator.

Yesterday, Today, Tomorrow

There are two days in every week about which we should not worry, two days which should be kept free from fear and apprehension.

One of these days is yesterday with its mistakes and cares, its faults and blunders, its aches and pains. Yesterday has passed forever beyond our control.

All the worry in the world cannot bring back yesterday. We cannot undo a single act we performed yesterday. We cannot erase a single word we said. Yesterday is gone.

It's not the experience of today that drives men mad - it is the remorse and bitterness for something which happened yesterday and the dread of what tomorrow may bring.

"Let us, therefore, live but one day at a time!"

From A.A. Beginner's
Pamphlet

3. AN "I MATTER" SELF-ESTEEM MEANS...
PUTTING FAILURES INTO PERSPECTIVE.

It was my first time to meet her family. They were all there - aunts, uncles, cousins, grandmas, the whole lot of them. I was a nervous wreck. It was a special occasion and everyone wanted to meet this guy Anne had been dating and talking so much about. We got up for dinner, loaded our plates and returned to our places in the living room where everyone ate from either their laps or portable folding TV tables. I was feeling uncomfortable enough to begin with when the absolute worst thing that could have happened, happened.

As I set my milk and dinner on the tray and pulled it closer - it toppled. Milk and meat spilt everywhere. One of the beets on my plate rolled clear across the room leaving a red trail on the pale green carpet. The room became deathly silent until one of Anne's young cousins asked his mother, in a voice loud enough for all to hear, "Why did he do that mom?"

I felt like a failure. I almost came to tears. I was only 18 or 19 at the time. I so wanted to be accepted by Anne and her family and I felt I had blown it by embarrassing myself and them.

Anne's mother is very clued in to how people feel. She could see I was devastated. Even though it was an accident, I took it personally and felt I really was the klutz everyone said I was. She pulled me aside and helped me tremendously by forcing me to put things into proper perspective.

What she did was insist that what had just happened was perfectly normal. It had nothing to do with me or their love and appreciation of me. She was also perceptive enough to insist I not tell anyone about what just happened.

"Just forget it ever happened", she said. For several years, I never told anyone about it. I never let that brief failure set me back. Because of the help of a caring lady, I put my "failures" into perspective.

Failure: the back door to success

By putting failure into perspective you are able to draw from the experiences of life and allow them to inspire, motivate and teach you instead of demoralize you. If you have had a personal failure you are not a failure. Many people experience disasters in their lives and take on the sense of being worthless because of it. If you have had something go wrong, perhaps a business, a sale, a relationship, a time others were depending on you and you blew it, don't think you are a failure. Perhaps you should take a closer look. If you've tried something that failed, don't feel you are a loser. Perhaps the problem isn't you but one of these:

Lack Of Experience

If you've tried something that failed don't think of yourself as a loser. It may just be that you lack experience. Take the first time I ever kissed a girl on the lips. I felt like a failure after that first kiss. You see - I missed. It was not a personal inadequacy, I just had no experience. (I've gotten much better since then by the way!)

Unrealistic Challenge

I've seen people try something great and give up trying after it fails. They are dejected and determined to play it safe from here on in. They take failure personally. At 21, I was the Vice President of a synthetic oil company for all of Canada. In a very short period of time, I realized it was not going to work. I lost money, prestige and a certain degree of confidence in myself. Then I discovered that I wasn't a failure, or a good-for-nothing businessman who was bound to fail. No, I was simply out of my league. I had taken on an unrealistic challenge.

Improper Training

Sales people across North America who hear my speeches and seminars want to know how to recover from rejection in the profession of selling. Some have blown a major account because they were put in a situation that was outside of their skill level and the result was a lost account. Is that person a failure? No way - they may not have been properly trained. You are not a failure. If you have had a similar experience, you are not a failure. You are still a champion. You may be in need of a training program, but you are still a champion.

4. AN "I MATTER" SELF-ESTEEM MEANS...
BEING PROUD OF WHO YOU ARE.

By putting failure and past events into perspective we are able to rise above embarrassments. We know that we have value regardless of the events of our lives.

There is nothing wrong with being proud to be Canadian, American, Chinese. I'm a French Canadian and proud of it. I'm a husband and a dad. I own my own company. I'm proud that I help people instead of hurting people.

Make a list of things you are proud of. You have a lot to be proud of. Are you honest? Are you warm, thoughtful and kind? Do you have a heritage to be proud of? Look long enough and you'll surprise yourself.

5. AN "I MATTER" SELF-ESTEEM MEANS...
YOU CHOOSE THE RIGHT VALUE SYSTEMS.

A self-esteem that says "I'm a worthwhile person" means I care enough about myself to stop comparing myself to wrong standards.

One foggy, cold, November night, the captain of a large ship saw what seemed like another ship's lights approaching. They indicated that there was about to be a head-on collision unless someone altered their course.

The captain quickly signalled via morse code, "Change your course 20 degrees to the south". The reply came blinking back, "you change your course 20 degrees to the north". Slightly offended, the captain pulled rank and indignantly replied to the other ship, "I am a sea captain with 22 years of experience you alter your course 20 degrees south". Without hesitation the signal flashed back, "I'm a seaman fourth class. You change your course 20 degrees north."

By this time the captain was furious and realizing the impending doom if one of them didn't alter their course fired off his final warning, "I'm a United States battleship, you change your course 20 degrees south". The final reply was this... "I'm a United States lighthouse - I suggest you alter your course 20 degrees north".

Like the captain of that battleship we have beliefs about ourselves, that are often based on wrong information. You may not need to alter your course at all! You may be going the right way. You may need to alter it 180 degrees. Either way, an "I matter" self-esteem says I will only judge myself with proper value standards.

Dr. Madison Sarratt, who taught mathematics at Vanderbilt University for many years, would admonish his class something like this before giving a test :

"Today I am giving two examinations; one in trigonometry and the other in honesty. I hope you will pass them both. If you must fail one, fail trigonometry. There are many good people in the world who can't pass trig, but there are no good people in the world who cannot pass the examination of honesty."

6. AN "I MATTER" SELF-ESTEEM MEANS...
LIVING BY THE DIAMOND PRINCIPLE.

Many people spend their whole lives searching for success when it is usually so close that they can reach out and touch it. Someone has said that "a diamond is a congealed drop of sunlight." That is you!!! Granted you may need forgiveness from God and man for past behaviour, but as a human being you are wonderful.

What are qualities of diamonds?

- **Durable**
- **Valuable**
- **Strong**

- Unique
- Precious
- Special
- Add to this list ...
-
-

These are some of the qualities of diamonds. Which one does not apply to a newborn baby, struggling salesman, wife longing for her husband's respect, a teenager giving in to drugs? The diamond describes mankind.

YOU ARE THE DIAMOND!

The Diamond Principle:

There resides within me the attributes of precious diamonds.
I am uniquely created. There is no other diamond quite like me.
I am precious. I have a sense of worth. I am priceless, I am valuable. I am lovable and capable.
Like a diamond, I reflect light bringing warmth and colour to all who see me.

Russell H. Conwell gave his speech "Acres of Diamonds" more than 5,000 times. The story illustrates how Ali Hafed sought riches and fame. He left his home and family to find a diamond mine. He sold his little farm and travelled to Palestine, Europe and at last all his money was spent. He was in rags, wretched and penniless.

He had spent everything in search of precious diamonds. Finally, he stood on the shores of a bay in Barcelona, Spain and when a great tide came in, he jumped in and was drowned.

One day, the man who purchased Ali Hafed's farm discovered something glimmering in the stream. It was a huge diamond. It was on this very farm that they discovered the diamond mine of Golconda. The largest diamonds on earth, including the Kohinoor and the Orloff from crown jewels of England came from that mine.

Had he stayed put and searched out the riches which were already in his possession Ali Hafed would have had Acres of Diamonds. He settled for Acres of Misery instead. If you want an "I matter" self-esteem begin where you are and what you are, unless where you are is causing you to feel terrible about what you are.

Self-esteem is not:

- Narcissism: "Ain't I enthralling."
- Bragging: "Look at how great I am."
- Arrogance: "I'm better than you."
- Self-centredness: "The whole world revolves around me."

THE "I MATTER" BUILDER KEYS

Key 1: Believe Correctly.

Chances are your childhood beliefs about Santa Claus, the tooth fairy and the Easter Bunny have changed. The evidence demanded that you alter your understanding. You could no longer believe in something that evidence disproved.

Subject your belief about yourself and your worth to a new set of evidence, one which affirms you as a unique diamond! There is a story which helped me adopt a new belief system about my worth. That story is the story of the prodigal son in the Bible. A son had squandered his inheritance and believed his father would reject him. He felt shame, guilt and worthlessness. Instead what he discovered was that he mattered to his father. You matter!!! You matter to God. Give up believing you don't matter; you do.

When the drill sergeant barked out, "Now, all you dumbbells fall out!", all but one recruit did so. Angered by what he thought was defiance, the sergeant marched up to the rookie and growled, "Well?" but the young man held his ground and said, "There certainly were a lot of them, weren't there sir?"

DO THIS

> Accept yourself
> Believe in yourself
> Compliment yourself
> Forgive yourself
> Reward yourself
> Discover yourself
> Acknowledge yourself
> Spiritualize yourself

Key 2: Befriend carefully

Befriend the right people: people who will build you up not bring you down. Bad company, simply put, leads to bad self-esteem.

At the recovery home for alcoholics and drug addicts where I lived and worked it was not uncommon for 3 or 4 people to have "slips" (fall off the wagon) at the same time. Misery does love company.

Examine who you befriend. Do they build you up or degrade you? Are they "put-down" experts? Do you feel worse about yourself after you've parted? If so, limit your exposure to those people. Choose instead to befriend those people who affirm your individuality, your worth, your qualities. Expose yourself to people who reflect back to you that you matter.

DO THIS

> Get to know important people.
> Write a note of appreciation to at least two people.
> Buy a millionaire dinner.
> Give of your time to a needy person.
> Avoid, if possible, people who do not value your worth.
> Find someone who needs a hug.
> Call a special person today.

Key 3: Behave Consistently

If you know you have high cholesterol and you continue to eat eggs every morning, what is your behaviour saying about your self-esteem? It would be saying something like this: "I don't matter a great deal or at all". Behave better and you'll feel better.

When we do the right things we feel better about ourselves. I don't want to over-emphasize this point to the level of reducing our lives to feelings. I'm not saying if it feels right do it. There are many things that feel right which are wrong.

Dr. Schuller once said that the greatest sin we can commit is one that causes us to say "I am unworthy". That's where this key kicks in. There are certain behaviours which cause us to think more highly of ourselves and other which make us feel shame and guilt. The latter should be avoided.

How do you feel about yourself when you are:

- caught in a lie
- suffering with a hangover
- stopped for speeding
- yelling at someone
- violating your sexual moral code
- 30 lbs overweight
- violating others
- gossiping
- trapped in a bad-habit

Behave consistently with your "I matter" beliefs about yourself. Dr. Phillip Johnson, the champion's consultant, says that one of the major issues which the world will have to deal with, along with the nuclear threat, the environment and globalization is the collapse of moral values. We lack systems which provide directions about how we behave. It will be of "crisis" proportion by the 21st century according to Dr. Johnson.

So we know that what we do and how we behave, can either build or harm our self-esteem. Why not practice some things which will make you have a strong appreciation of yourself?

DO THIS

- Set a goal and accomplish it.
- Change your posture.
- Stand with confidence.
- Do something nice for someone and tell no one.
- Have dinner at an expensive restaurant.
- Tackle a creative project.
- Join a status-building organization that commands respect in your community.
- Build someone else's self-esteem.
- Tell others they matter.
- Find a pen pal in prison.
- Do something you've always wanted to do and don't feel guilty.

In summary, my message of hope is this:

YOU MATTER!!!

Remember this: what you believe in your heart about yourself is what you are. You can change your belief. You need to continue believing in yourself. You matter!!! Watch who you befriend, stick with those who affirm your worth and correct any negative or damaging behaviour. Do only those things which are consistent with your belief about yourself.

CHAPTER 3

THE PRACTICE OF SUCCESSIBILITY THINKING

Successibility Thinking is an attitude that refuses to quit, actions that relentlessly build and beliefs that constantly affirm; putting all of life in proper perspective.

> Success + Possibility = Successibility Thinking

Everyone knows that habits are not easily broken and that every great motivational breakthrough requires hard work. Are you willing to commit yourself to a program of Successibility Thinking development? You can re-program yourself for success by spending 10 minutes a day working on your greatest asset - your mind.

For years, leaders in the field of human potential development have espoused the use of affirmations. Affirmations are things you say to yourself about yourself; a form of re-programming your mind. They help you change your attitude and perspective in life. Believe the experts; affirmations really work.

THE 31 SUCCESSIBILITY THINKING DECLARATIONS

ONE
FOR EVERYDAY OF THE MONTH

Instructions:

1. Read one Declaration each day. There are 31, one for each day of the month.

2. Read it silently a few times putting feeling and conviction into it.

3. Read it out loud 10 times now and 10 times throughout the day. (Write them on 3 x 5 cards or purchase the Successibility Thinking Declaration card pack).

4. Follow the SUCCESS BUILDER PROJECTS instructions. Someone once said, "Instruction without application only leads to frustration."

5. Put a check mark beside the SUCCESS BUILDER PROJECT which you have completed.

DECLARATION #1

I MATTER

> I MATTER TO MYSELF AND OTHERS. I AM A SIGNIFICANT PERSON WITH INCREDIBLE POTENTIAL AND ABILITIES. I AM AWARE OF MY FLAWS AND CHOOSE TO APPRECIATE MYSELF EVEN WITH THEM. I LOVE MYSELF.

SUCCESS BUILDER PROJECT:

Make a list of ten things that make you unique.

1.

2.

3.

4.

5.

6.

7.

8.

9.

10.

DECLARATION #2

I CAN BECAUSE I THINK I CAN

I CAN BECAUSE I THINK I CAN. I AM PROGRAMMED FOR SUCCESS. I BELIEVE I AM A WINNER! THERE IS NOTHING I CAN'T DO. MY BELIEF SYSTEMS SAYS THERE ARE NO LIMITS. I CAN! I CAN! I CAN!

SUCCESS BUILDER PROJECT:

Find one thing in your life you felt was impossible or you gave up trying. Set a goal in this area and commit yourself to succeed at it using this Declaration.

DECLARATION #3

I DON'T FEAR FAILURE

I DON'T FEAR FAILURE. I'M NOT AFRAID TO RISK, OR TO TAKE CHANCES. I AM A PERSON OF GREAT COURAGE. I WOULD RATHER TRY AND POSSIBLY FAIL, THAN SUCCEED IN DOING NOTHING.

SUCCESS BUILDER PROJECT:

Read, listen to tapes or discuss with a colleague the advantages of not fearing failure today.

DECLARATION #4

I DELETE THE WORD "IMPOSSIBLE"

> I DELETE THE WORD "IMPOSSIBLE" FROM MY MEMORY BANK. I HAVE LITTLE OR NO USE FOR SUCH A WORD. THE SAME APPLIES TO WORDS LIKE: FAILURE, CAN'T, NO WAY, NEVER. INSIDE MY INTERNAL COMPUTER I PERFORM "SEARCH AND REPLACE" FUNCTIONS, ADOPTING THEIR OPPOSITES INSTEAD.

SUCCESS BUILDER PROJECT:

Every time you hear the word "impossible" today gently bite the tip of your tongue. This will provide a vivid illustration of just how prevalent the word is used.

DECLARATION #5

TODAY MARKS A NEW BEGINNING

> TODAY MARKS A NEW BEGINNING FOR ME. I START AFRESH TODAY! I DO AWAY WITH THE GARMENTS OF MY PAST WITH ALL THEIR DOUBTS, STRUGGLES AND CONCERNS. PEOPLE WILL SEE A NEW ME.

SUCCESS BUILDER PROJECT:

List anything in your past that still haunts, worries or causes you shame or embarrassment. Put a big X though the list and set the paper on fire.

DECLARATION #6

MY ENTHUSIASM IS OVERFLOWING

> MY ENTHUSIASM IS OVERFLOWING. I'M AN "UP" PERSON. MY ATTITUDE IS CONTAGIOUS, OTHERS LOOK TO ME TO RAISE MORALE. I AM DYNAMIC.

SUCCESS BUILDER PROJECT:

Today, every time you talk on the telephone, shake someone's hand, or meet people, do it with more energy than before. Note their reactions.

DECLARATION#7

I REJECT NEGATIVE SELF-TALK

> **I REJECT NEGATIVE SELF-TALK. I APPRECIATE MYSELF. I SAY THINGS TO MYSELF THAT BUILD ME UP. I HAVE MANY STRENGTHS, ABILITIES, QUALITIES AND POTENTIAL. THIS IS WHAT I FOCUS ON.**

SUCCESS BUILDER PROJECT:

What do you appreciate about yourself? Make a list of 30 things and save the list for review on the 7th of each month.

1.	2.
3.	4.
5.	6.
7.	8.
9.	10.
11.	12
13.	14.
15.	16.
17.	18.
19.	20.
21.	22.
23.	24.
25.	26.
27.	28.
29.	30.

DECLARATION #8

I AM HAPPY

I AM HAPPY! I ENJOY A GOOD LIFE. REGARDLESS OF THE STORMS AND PROBLEMS OF LIFE, I AM HAPPY. JOY IS WITHIN ME EVEN IN THE MIDST OF THE COLD, HARD WINTERS OF LIFE. THERE IS WITHIN ME AN INVINCIBLE SUMMER.

SUCCESS BUILDER PROJECT:

What would a happy person say to himself? If you were full of joy what would your self-talk be? Regardless of how you presently feel, repeat those things to yourself, out loud right now.

DECLARATION#9

I NEVER GIVE-UP

> I NEVER GIVE-UP! I AM NOT A QUITTER. I PERSIST UNTIL I SUCCEED. I AM PROGRAMMED FOR SUCCESS. I AM MADE OF THE "RIGHT STUFF". NO MATTER WHAT - I NEVER STOP TRYING. I WIN.

SUCCESS BUILDER PROJECT:

Buy the classic book, <u>THE GREATEST SALESMAN IN THE WORLD</u> by Og Mandino and read pages 63 to 67. It will revolutionize your life.

DECLARATION #10

MY MIND IS POSITIVE TODAY.

I WILL FILL MY MIND WITH SOMETHING POSITIVE TODAY. I LOVE TO READ AND LISTEN TO POSITIVE INSPIRATION, MOTIVATION AND TRAINING. I TAKE THE TIME TO IN-PUT GREAT, SUCCESSIBILITY THINKING IDEAS INTO MY MIND. I DESERVE THIS INFORMATION.

SUCCESS BUILDER PROJECT:

Adopt a slogan as your motto for the year. "What the mind can conceive and believe it can achieve", is an example of a classic. Find your own. Write it below.

My success slogan for this year is...

DECLARATION #11

NOBODY'S PERFECT

> NOBODY'S PERFECT - MYSELF IN-CLUDED. EVERYONE HAS FLAWS AND PROBLEMS. I ACCEPT MYSELF, MY BODY, MY IMPERFECTIONS. I FIX THOSE THINGS I CAN AND EMBRACE THOSE THINGS THAT ARE OUT-SIDE OF MY CONTROL. I LOVE AND ACCEPT MYSELF.

SUCCESS BUILDER PROJECT:

Repeat the Serenity Prayer

"God grant me the serenity
To accept the things I can't change
The courage to change the things I can
And the wisdom to know the difference."

DECLARATION #12

I AM A PERSON OF PASSION

> I AM A PERSON OF PASSION AND COMMITMENT. I SUCCEED BECAUSE I AM INTENSELY DEDICATED TO ACHIEVEMENT. I REJECT MEDIOCRITY AND AM WILLING TO STICK AT THINGS UNTIL I PROSPER BECAUSE I AM SO PASSIONATE ABOUT MYSELF AND MY POTENTIAL.

SUCCESS BUILDER PROJECT:

Make a list of at least 5 things you would be willing to die for. That is your passion. Expand the list to include what you would do if you knew you could not fail and money was not an issue.

1.

2.

3.

4.

5.

DECLARATION #13

I LIVE OUT THE DIAMOND PRINCIPLE

I LIVE OUT THE DIAMOND PRINCIPLE. IT SAYS "RESIDING WITHIN ME ARE THE ATTRIBUTES OF PRECIOUS DIAMONDS. LIKE THE DIAMOND, I AM UNIQUELY CREATED. THERE IS NO OTHER DIAMOND QUITE LIKE ME.

I AM PRECIOUS. I HAVE A SENSE OF WORTH. I AM PRICELESS. I AM VALUABLE. I AM LOVEABLE AND CAPABLE.

LIKE A DIAMOND I REFLECT LIGHT, BRINGING WARMTH AND COLOUR TO ALL WHO SEE ME."

SUCCESS BUILDER PROJECT:

Find an encyclopedia that discusses the properties of diamonds. Make a list, as large as you can, describing the qualities and attributes of diamonds. They will all apply directly to you. You are a diamond of a person.

DECLARATION #14

I THINK BIG

> I THINK BIG. I REFUSE TO PLACE LIMITS ON MY IMAGINATION. I WILL ACCOMPLISH MORE IN THIS LIFE THAN I EVER PREVIOUSLY DREAMED POSSIBLE. I AM A "NO-LIMITS" PERSON. I STRETCH MYSELF ALL THE TIME. I MAXIMIZE MY FULL POTENTIAL.

SUCCESS BUILDER PROJECT:

Write down four aspirations you hope to accomplish in the next five years. For the sake of this application, double each aspiration. How would you feel if you indeed accomplished double? Now why not shoot for the higher goals?

1.   1.

2.   2.

3.   3.

4.   4.

DECLARATION #15

I REGULARLY ASK FOR HELP

> I REGULARLY ASK FOR HELP. I'M NOT TOO PROUD TO SEEK ASSISTANCE. IN FACT, ONE OF THE GREAT ASSETS I HAVE IS MY ABILITY TO LEARN FROM OTHERS. I AM HUMBLE ENOUGH TO SHUT-UP AND LISTEN TO ADVICE. I AM CONFIDENT ENOUGH TO TAKE CRITICISM WITHOUT IT AFFECTING MY SELF-ESTEEM.

SUCCESS BUILDER PROJECT:

Identify a high achiever from whom you could learn something, perhaps a leader in your company, industry or community. Make an appointment with them. Buy them lunch and prepare a list of five questions for them to answer which would help you.

I set a goal to meet these five people:

1.

2.

3.

4.

5.

DECLARATION #16

MY PHYSIOLOGY IS GOOD

MY PHYSIOLOGY CONVEYS CONFIDENCE, ENERGY, POWER AND SUCCESS. MY BODY SPEAKS OF MY SURETY, POTENCY, VIGOUR AND TRIUMPH. I AM RELAXED, POISED AND ENERGIZED. MY EYES, HANDS, POSTURE, VOICE AND BREATHING ALL SPEAK OF MY INTERNAL STATE OF CONTROL AND RESOURCEFULNESS.

SUCCESS BUILDER PROJECT:

Stand erect, look up with your eyes wide open. Make an expression of GREAT JOY with your face. Put on huge smile, breathe deeply and slam your hands together in applause and shout, "Man, am I depressed today". You will find that it's impossible to be depressed in that physiology.

DECLARATION #17

ALL STORMS PASS

ALL STORMS PASS. INDEED, EVERY PROBLEM HAS A LIMITED DURATION. HASSLES DO END. PROBLEMS ARE NOT PERMANENT. THE COLD OF WINTER INEVITABLY BRINGS WITH IT THE THAW OF SPRING AND THE WARMTH OF SUMMER. I WILL SURVIVE THE STORMS OF LIFE. I AM STRONG! I'LL OUTLAST THE CHALLENGES LIFE BRINGS TO ME.

SUCCESS BUILDER PROJECT:

If you believe this principle share it with someone today. Find someone who is going through a valley right now. Remind them that life can be hard but that all problems cease. With the valleys come the mountain tops. Clouds will give way to sunshine.

DECLARATION #18

I WILL MAKE IT - NO MATTER WHAT

I WILL MAKE IT NO MATTER WHAT. I AM
CONVINCED THAT I AM A PRIME PERFORMER
RIGHT NOW. I AM A SUCCESSIBILITY
THINKER! SUCCESS IS NOT A DESTINATION,
IT'S A JOURNEY. THEREFORE, I'LL PERSIST NO
MATTER WHAT.

SUCCESS BUILDER PROJECT:

Is there anything in your past that you gave-up trying? If there
is, re-flame the fires by committing yourself to apply this declaration to it. Take action this week.

DECLARATION #19

I AM IN CONTROL OF MY FEELINGS

> I AM IN CONTROL OF MY FEELINGS. I CONFRONT NEGATIVE FEELINGS. I EASILY REMOVE SUCH UNDESIRABLE EMOTIONS AS SELF-PITY, ANGER, FEAR, DEPRESSION AND HATRED. I AM A STRONG, BALANCED AND CONTROLLED INDIVIDUAL. I AM IN-CHARGE OF MY EMOTIONS. THEY DON'T CONTROL ME.

SUCCESS BUILDER PROJECT:

Make a list of all the emotions which you have experienced during this past week. After listing all recallable emotions, list the emotions under one of these three categories: Desirable, Undesirable or Difficult to Categorize. Now come up with practical solutions as to how you could have turned the Undesirable emotions around.

DECLARATION #20

TODAY MAY BE MY LAST

TODAY MAY BE MY LAST THEREFORE I
WILL LIVE IT SO. I KNOW WHAT'S REALLY IM-
PORTANT TO ME IN LIFE. I VALUE RELATION-
SHIPS, I PUT INCOME, POSSESSIONS, CAREER,
AND EVEN SUCCESS IN PROPER PERSPECTIVE.
I LIVE MY LIFE FOR WHAT IS IMPORTANT, NOT
FOR WHAT IS URGENT.

SUCCESS BUILDER PROJECT:

What are your governing values? If you only had two years to
live what would you do differently? Perhaps you do only have
two years or maybe even two months, maybe even two days. Is
there anything you should re-prioritize? Is there someone you
should talk to, apologize to, share your love with? Do it!!!

DECLARATION #21

IF IT'S GOING TO BE - IT'S UP TO ME

> IF IT'S GOING TO BE - IT'S UP TO ME. I MAKE THINGS HAPPEN. I AM TOTALLY RESPONSIBLE! I DO NOT WAIT FOR ANYONE TO SOLVE MY PROBLEMS, MAKE MY LIFE EASIER OR CREATE MY SUCCESS. I SEEK ASSISTANCE, THAT'S FOR SURE, BUT I NEVER ABDICATE MY LEADERSHIP ROLE IN SEEING MY DREAMS COME TRUE. I AM NOT A VICTIM OF CIRCUMSTANCES.

SUCCESS BUILDER PROJECT:

Read the chapter, The Seven Lies of Success in Anthony Robbins' book, Unlimited Power, pages 69 to 82.

DECLARATION #22

I REJECT THE CONCEPT OF FAILURE

> I REJECT THE CONCEPT OF FAILURE. THERE REALLY ISN'T SUCH A THING. MY BELIEF IS THAT I LEARN AND GROW WITH EVERY EVENT OF LIFE. I SUCCEED BECAUSE I DEVELOP. SUCCESS IS AN ATTITUDE NOT AN ACTION. IT'S AN OUTLOOK, A MIND-SET AND I POSSESS IT, RIGHT HERE AND NOW.

SUCCESS BUILDER PROJECT:

Think of a personal "failure" in your life. What have you learned as a result of it? Make a list of all the good things that have come as a result of that event. Would you still call it a "failure". Determine that you are presently a winner. You are!!!

DECLARATION #23

I GIVE TO OTHERS

> **I GIVE TO OTHERS THAT WHICH I HAVE ABUNDANTLY RECEIVED. TO KEEP WHAT I HAVE I MUST GIVE IT AWAY. I AM A GRATEFUL PERSON. I HAVE RECEIVED SO MUCH IN LIFE AND NOW PASS SOME OF IT BACK TO OTHERS. I KNOW THAT FOR ME TO KEEP SOMETHING I MUST GIVE IT AWAY. I DO SO FREELY AND GENEROUSLY.**

SUCCESS BUILDER PROJECT:

What organization have you benefitted the most from? Decide today how you can show your gratitude to them. The master was very correct when He stated; "What you sow, you reap". Show how grateful you are by doing more than you have in the past.

I plan to donate (time, money, or advice) to following organizations this year:

DECLARATION #24

THERE ARE NO PROBLEMS

THERE ARE NO PROBLEMS ONLY A SHORTAGE OF IDEAS. I REFUSE TO LOOK AT OBSTACLES AS PROBLEMS. I AM SOLUTION ORIENTATED NOT PROBLEM ORIENTATED. I AM A CREATIVE PERSON THEREFORE INGENIOUS CONCEPTS COME TO ME TO REMOVE ALL SUCCESS-BLOCKERS. FOR ME THE ISSUE IS IDEAS NOT PROBLEMS.

SUCCESS BUILDER PROJECT:

Apply the P.A.P.A. Problem Solving Principles to any problem you are facing right now.

P.: Problem Scope: List the scope of the problem you are facing now. It may be helpful to break it down or categorize it.

A.: Apply Creativity: List possible solutions without evaluating their viability. Create a long list of alternatives.

P.: Produce Synonyms: Now take that list and come up with one synonym for each item on the list. This will multiply your creative solutions.

A.: Act.: Decide to act. Pick only two solutions first. Take the two ideas with the greatest potential and try to solve them by going down every possible street until you have travelled down every dead end. Repeat the whole process until you receive the winning idea.

DECLARATION #25

I INVEST IN MYSELF

I INVEST IN MYSELF. I AM WORTH IT. MY PERSONAL DEVELOPMENT IS VERY IMPORTANT IN MY LIFE. UNLIKE THE MASSES, I DO NOT QUIVER AT THE THOUGHT OF MONETARY OR TIME INVESTMENTS. I CAN HANDLE THE INVESTMENT PHASE IN ORDER TO REAP THE BENEFIT PHASE LATER. LIKE A CHAMPION ATHLETE WHO TRAINS RELENTLESSLY, I TOO AM WILLING TO PAY THE PRICE TO BE THE BEST.

SUCCESS BUILDER PROJECT:

Decide to attend a personal development seminar. Purchase some powerful motivational tapes. Buy a book which will help you feel better about yourself and will provide insight into your development. Don't be afraid to treat yourself to something today.

The areas I would like to invest in my human potential are:

DECLARATION #26

I'M A WORTHWHILE PERSON

I'M A WORTHWHILE PERSON. I HAVE A STRONG SENSE OF WORTH AND IT IS SO REGARDLESS OF WHAT ANYONE SAYS ABOUT ME, THINKS OF ME OR DOES TO ME. I AM CAREFULLY AND WONDERFULLY CREATED. I AM FREE FROM THE DESPERATE NEED FOR APPROVAL. I AM OF WORTH, PERIOD. I MAT-TER.

SUCCESS BUILDER PROJECT:

Repeat this affirmation at least 100 times today.

"I'M A WORTHWHILE PERSON NO MATTER WHAT YOU THINK, SAY OR DO TO ME"

DECLARATION #27

I'LL TREAT MYSELF

> I'LL TREAT MYSELF TO SOMETHING SPECIAL TODAY. I'M OF ENOUGH VALUE TO DO NICE THINGS FOR MYSELF. SELF-DENIAL IS GREAT WHEN USED FOR THE SAKE OF OTHERS, BUT NEVER AS A REFLECTION OF MY WORTH. THEREFORE I WILL DO SOMETHING PLEASURABLE JUST FOR ME.

SUCCESS BUILDER PROJECT:

Give yourself a treat today without feeling guilty. Go get a massage or a facial. Buy yourself a new suit. Take the phone off the hook and have a rest. Take a holiday. Go out to an exclusive restaurant. Rent a limousine and go to the theatre. The key is don't feel guilty. You will feel great.

DECLARATION #28

I CHOOSE YES YES LIVING

I CHOOSE YES YES INSTEAD OF NO NO LIVING. I AM AN ETERNAL OPTIMIST. I REFUSE TO DWELL ON THE NEGATIVES IN LIFE. I CHOOSE RATHER TO SEE THE BRIGHT SIDE OF LIFE TODAY. I CHOOSE TO ACCEN-TUATE THE POSITIVE. THIS OPTIMISM MAKES ME ATTRACTIVE TO THOSE AROUND ME. EVERYTHING AROUND ME MAY BE SHOUTING NO NO, BUT I ALWAYS EMBRACE YES YES.

SUCCESS BUILDER PROJECT:

There is a positive side to every negative. Read the newspaper and re-write a negative story in positive terms. It is possible. Forty percent chance of rain can be re-written as sixty percent chance of sunshine. It's the same thing except one focuses on rain, the other sunshine. Successibility Thinkers prefer sunshine to rain.

DECLARATION #29

I DON'T MIND PAYING THE PRICE

I DON'T MIND PAYING THE PRICE FOR SUCCESS. I KNOW THAT TO ACHIEVE MUCH, ONE MUST PAY MUCH. I AM WILLING TO MAKE SACRIFICES IN ORDER TO SEE MY DREAMS COME TO REALITY. I ACCEPT THE PRINCIPLE OF DELAYED GRATIFICATION. I DON'T NEED "INSTANT" ANYTHING, I CAN HANDLE PAYING NOW TO ENJOY LATER.

SUCCESS BUILDER PROJECT:

The principle of delayed gratification is one whereby we count on and even schedule the investment or pain phase first in order to more fully enjoy the pleasure phase later. It's getting the hard work done first to reap the enjoyment later. What great pleasure or accomplishment do you want in life? It's nothing more than a wishy washy dream unless you begin now working on and scheduling the effort required to see it come to pass. Write a schedule of what it will take for you to accomplish it.

DECLARATION #30

I COUNT MY BLESSINGS EVERYDAY

> I COUNT MY BLESSINGS EVERYDAY. I REALIZE HOW FORTUNATE I AM. I DO NOT TAKE ANYTHING FOR GRANTED. I AM RICHLY BLESSED AND I AM THANKFUL FOR THIS FACT. I REJECT SELF-PITY AND REFUSE TO GRUMBLE ABOUT MY LOT IN LIFE. THINGS ARE GOING GREAT WITH ME.

SUCCESS BUILDER PROJECT:

What are you thankful for? Chances are people feature highly in your answer to that question. Why not tell the ones you love that you love them today. Tell them you count them as one of your greatest blessings.

DECLARATION #31

I DON'T SWEAT THE SMALL STUFF

I DON'T SWEAT THE SMALL STUFF AND IT'S ALL SMALL STUFF. THESE ARE THE TWO RULES OF SUCCESSIBILITY THINKING. I HAVE AN AMAZING RESILIENCE. I SEE LIFE, PROBLEMS AND CHALLENGES FOR WHAT THEY ARE. I AM NOT EASILY TOPPLED. I CAN HANDLE LIFE. I AM A PERSON OF GREAT COURAGE AND CONFIDENCE.

SUCCESS BUILDER PROJECT:

Share the two rules of Successibility Thinking with at least one person today.

CONCLUSION

Take the time, make the time, invest the time to make these Successibility Thinking Declarations part of your life. Begin the practice of conquering the Motivational Success Blockers by developing the habit of doing your daily Declarations.

Dr. Kenneth McFarland shares a fascinating story about Tommy McReynold. Tommy was called "The Rope". He got that nickname because he managed to rope the whole community together in the spirit of involvement and togetherness. He did that by being a star athlete on the basketball court. Tommy broke all the local, state and national scoring records. His team was winning all the games.

Tragically, "The Rope" was killed instantly in an automobile accident. Dr. McFarland shares that when he arrived at the stricken home, Papa McReynold said to him, as he showed him Tommy's closet, "We've got a saying down here, that when we lose a young'en, we hang our dreams in the closet."

It must have taken some courage but Dr. McFarland confronted the saddened father's erroneous thinking. "That doesn't sound right, Papa McReynold. You should never hang your dreams in the closet." Papa replied, "Ken, I know you love me because you wouldn't be here at 3:00 a.m. if you didn't. But my boy won't be going to school tomorrow morning. At Christmas his presents won't get opened. Next Thanksgiving, he won't be enjoying turkey with us. No, we hang our dreams in the closet."

Just then Tommy's younger brother Lance entered the room. "You're not going to hang your dreams in the closet are you, Lance?" asked Dr. McFarland. With a tinge of courage the reply came back, "No sir. Thank you sir." It was as if he really meant it.

Several years had past when the great orator McFarland, was invited back to that community to be the guest of honour for special festivities. Their local basketball team was to play in the finals against their long-time rivals.

After giving an after-dinner speech Dr. McFarland watched what he said was one of the most exciting games of his life. Many records were broken that night, many of the records which were held by Tommy, "The Rope". The game went right down to the wire. The opposing team were one point ahead with less than a minute to play. They were winning 53 to 52. They were going to lose by one point. As the gun was set to go off, a skinny kid shot through the crowd and let a long shot go from several feet away. He sunk it! They had won the game! The atmosphere was so charged that the winning supporters gathered at centre court to hug, cheer and celebrate the victory.

Dr. McFarland continued, "Some were huggin', some were kissin', some were taking advantage of the situation, then I felt the strong arms of Papa McReynold hug me tight. With tears streaming down his cheeks, Tommy's dad said, 'I guess you were right - we shouldn't hang our dreams in the closet."

You see the person who had broken all of Tommy's previously held records and shot the winning basket was none other than Lance, Tommy's younger brother." What Dr. Kenneth McFarland relayed to a grieving father, I want to pass on to you too. NEVER HANG YOUR DREAMS IN THE CLOSET!

---◆---

CONQUERING
THE
DIRECTIONAL
SUCCESS-BLOCKERS

---◆---

CHAPTER 4

Ready, Fire, Aim!
Keys to Successful
Goal Setting

Helen Keller was once asked, "Is there anything worse than being blind?" She replied, "Yes. The most pathetic person in the world is someone who has sight but no vision."

Ms. Keller was very perceptive. Many people have aspirations and dreams but prefer to sit, and do nothing instead of planning their fulfilment.

We have the power to control our destiny. The key is having goals and setting them well enough and tracking them diligently enough to see them come to fruition.

Ask any psychiatrist if patients on psychiatric wards have clearly defined goals and know exactly what they want out of life. I think you can imagine what the answer would be. Now ask the manager of a top producing sales force the same question. You will discover that the most successful people in business and in life practice goal setting as a regular part of living.

In his book, <u>Man's Search for Meaning</u>, Victor Frankl, successor of Sigmund Freud, argues that the "loss of hope and courage can have a deadly effect on man." As a result of his experiences in a Nazi concentration camp, Frankl contends that when a man no longer possesses a motive for living, no future to look toward, he curls up in a corner and dies. "Any attempt to restore a man's inner strength in camp", he writes, "had first to succeed in showing him some future goal." If I have no intention of spending time on a psychiatric ward but do want to be counted as a high achiever in life, it makes good sense to set goals like the winners do!

We live in a busy world. Many people confuse activity with accomplishment. Many of us are so busy we find it difficult to stop long enough to ponder such things. Let's face it. We can never achieve success in life without first considering where we want to go. We wouldn't set sail on the ocean hoping to get somewhere, or just anywhere.

Bishop Fulton Sheen was to speak in a city he had never previously visited. He was running late and wasn't sure of his directions. He stopped to ask a group of kids if they could direct him to the city hall. After they gave him the information he requested, they asked why he was going there. He said that he was going to give a speech on how to get to heaven. Being a good Bishop, he asked if they would like to come along and hear his speech. "No thanks," said one youngster, "you don't even know how to get to city hall."

Why Set Goals?

The FBI went into one town to investigate the work of what appeared to be a sharpshooter. They were amazed to find many bulls-eyes drawn on various targets with bullets that had penetrated the exact centre of the targets. When they finally found the man who had been doing the shooting, they asked him what his secret was.

The answer was simple: he shot the bullet first, and drew the bulls-eye later. In application: do we allow our activities to determine our goals, or do we have our goals determine our activities?

A bumper sticker read: "Don't follow me. I'm lost too". Motion does not always mean direction.

GOALS

They keep you focused.

They give you something to shoot for.

They keep solution ideas flowing.

They give you enthusiasm.

They chart your course in life.

They give you purpose.

They help you stay productive.

They give you clarity in decision making.

They provide a measuring stick for considering ideas.

They help you stay organized.

They help you sell yourself to others.

They help you judge your productivity and effectiveness.

They will make your boss happy.

Types of Goals

During my seminars and speeches people often ask me if goals should be "realistic". I say of course that they should unless "unrealistic" is just a disguise for limitation thinking.

Someone said "Goals should be within our grasp but just outside our reach." It has to be big enough to excite us but not too challenging to squash us. Believable and achievable is the way to set goals. In addition, Mark Victor Hansen said that we can never have too many goals.

Short-term Goals: What do you want to achieve in the next 3 to 6 months?

Mid-term Goals: These are goals you want to accomplish within 6 to 12 months.

Long-term Goals: For many of us these are goals we set for the next 3 to 5 years. There was a day when long-term planning meant planning for 10 to 20 years. I'm afraid our times have changed too much. Consider goals dealing with longer than 5 years in the next category.

Lifetime goals: These goals are set by asking, "When I'm 90 years old what would I like to have accomplished?" What would I like to be remembered for?

Dr. Anthony Campolo, a dynamic sociology professor, on one of his films shares the results of a survey where 50 people 95 years and older were asked: "If you could live your life over again what would you do differently?". The answers surprised me. These old folks said that if they could live their lives over again they would...

1. Reflect more. Take the time to think about what was going on and live their lives along well thought out priorities. They would contemplate the meaning of life, family, work much more.

2. Risk more. These wonderful aged human beings said they would have taken more chances in life. If they could re-live their lives they wouldn't be so scared to risk. They would have developed more courage to venture out of their comfort zones.

3. Do things that would out-last them. They wanted to know that their lives counted for something, that long after they left this world, somehow their impact would live on. We all can learn something from these people about setting goals. Consider what they said as you set the course for your life.

CATEGORIES OF GOALS

Vocational

What goals do you want to reach in this area? A raise? A promotion? Would you like to win some award or special recognition? Where do you see your career going? Would you like to change your career?

Financial

How much money do you desire? What will your bank account or investments be like in the future? Would you like to make a million dollars? Would you like to own more real estate? What will your annual income be in five years? When will you build the new wing down at the cancer hospital?

Social

Which organizations will you join? What will your social life be like in the future? Would you like new relationships? Would you like to make improvements in this area? What kind of a friend will you be to others?

Physical

What state will your body be in next year at this time? If you plan to lose weight - how much? When? Would you like to eat better? Would you like to have more energy? Going to start exercising soon? When? Where? With who?

Mental

How will you develop your mind? What would you like to learn more than anything else? Can you think of some books you would like to read or courses you would like to take? What will it be? Memory training? Public speaking? New language?

Family

What would you like to change at home? Are you spending quality time developing solid relationships? What goals do you have for your family life? What trips, events, plans will make you richer on the family side of life?

Spiritual

What aspect of your spiritual life will you develop? Have you sensed a certain emptiness that spiritual development may solve? What will you do about it? What will your involvement be in spiritual organizations?

CONSIDER ALSO...

Character Goals

Your ideal is what you wish you were

Your reputation is what people say you are

Your character is what you are

It seems in our day, character qualities like honesty, ethics, loyalty, kindness, love, meekness, charity are almost discouraged.

Someone once said, "If we sow a thought, we reap an act; If we sow an act, we reap a habit; If we sow a habit, we reap a character; If we sow a character, we reap a destiny."

Is there a particular character trait you would like to develop? Perhaps you would like to become more patient, or increase your appreciation of others. Set character goals.

Breakthrough Goals

These goals concern themselves with breaking through some aspect of our being. Breakthrough goals are things you become. Making a decision to never repeat a certain mistake or changing your attitude from negative to positive are examples of breakthrough goals. You break through one way of doing something to another way.

Habit Breaking Goals

Overheard at a party: "One time I gave up drinking, smoking and chasing women all at once. It was the worst twenty minutes of my life."

Have you wanted to stop doing something for ages? How

long have you wanted to quit drinking? Or smoking? Why not set a goal to break those habits? Bad habits are like comfortable beds; easy to get into but hard to get out of. It is highly unlikely that you will just wake up some morning and the habit will be gone. Plan habit breaking goals now.

Adventure Goals

Jump out of a plane - with a parachute of course! Now there is an adventure goal; Take a trip through Europe on a motorcycle. Learn to mountain climb. Start a business. Attend a firewalk seminar. Have a baby. "A baby", someone has said, "is an elongated intestinal tract with a loud noise at one end and no responsibility at the other." What exciting thing keeps you awake at night but you have never had the courage to do it? Set a goal and go after it.

"Far better it is to dare mighty things, to win glorious triumphs, even though checkered by failure, than to take rank with those poor spirits who neither enjoy much nor suffer much because they live in the grey twilight that knows neither victory nor defeat."

President Roosevelt

Stress Reduction Goals

You are at a busy intersection, you are running late, the light turns green but you can't pass because cars block the intersection. You fume! Now there's a place to set stress reduction goals - in traffic. Where else could you reduce stress in your life? Why not give it some thought.

KEYS TO GOAL SETTING
THE "HOW TO'S "

Key #1

IT MUST BE WRITTEN AND IT MUST BE SPECIFIC

To say you want to be rich or happily married is more of a wish than a goal. For a goal to be effective you must describe, in detail what it will look like.

If I set a goal to be a millionaire, I need to describe that goal in measurable terminology. What will my bank account look like? What car will I drive? Some experts say you should go as far as to describe the colour of the car.

Use what behaviourial scientist Dr. Robert Mager calls the "Daddy Test". Write the goal and say - Daddy come watch me ... (state the goal). If Daddy would know exactly what you are doing then it passes the Daddy Test.

For example, "Daddy, come watch me be a millionaire." Daddy would not know exactly what that means. Now if I re-wrote the goal and said, "Daddy, come watch me pay cash for a new red Rolls Royce", Daddy would know exactly what I would be doing - therefore it is a clearly written goal.

Key #2

IT MUST HAVE A DEADLINE

Deadlines scare some people away from goal setting. Will I feel like a failure if I don't reach it on time? Not to worry. Perhaps the date is wrong. It can be changed, but setting a deadline does provide something for you to shoot for.

In addition to achievement deadlines, you should consider breaking down the goal into smaller pieces and setting milestones. Milestones are indicators along the way which will help you track your progress.

If you set a goal to lose 25 lbs. in 10 months, you could date a goal for each of the 10 months. In the first month you should have dropped 2.5 lbs., the same the second, third and so on. Isn't it easier to break it down and set shorter deadlines? Anyone can lose 2.5 lbs. in a month. If you broke it down even further that would mean losing less than half a pound a week. Robert Schuller says:

> "Yard by yard, life is hard; but by the inch, it's a cinch."

Key #3

IT MUST IDENTIFY THE POTENTIAL SUCCESS - BLOCKERS

You can count on obstacles. You'd better count on them! Anything worthwhile in life will have a cost, a price to pay and hurdles to conquer. Successful goal setters identify those potential problems first before they encounter them. This puts them in a much stronger position to overcome them.

Last year I set a goal to lose 25 lbs. I considered the Success-Blockers; the obstacles that would attempt to block my achieving the goal. For me, the obstacles to that goal are the fact that I hate exercise and love food. I travel a lot and spend time in fine hotels. I'm not the type of person who can travel on a plane all night, get to my hotel room at midnight, and order a salad from room service, particularly if there is prime rib and cheese cake on the same menu.

That was a potential obstacle for me. Considering this ahead of time allowed me to plan how to handle the obstacle when faced with it. It didn't always work! I'm a sucker for cheese cake!

Key #4

IT MUST INCLUDE A LIST OF SKILLS YOU WILL NEED TO DEVELOP TO ACHIEVE THE GOAL

If you set a goal to sail around the world you might have to develop some navigational skills. It probably would help. If you want to write a book you may need to develop grammatical skills. What this key does is force you to consider ahead of time the tools you will need in order to see your dreams come true. Make a list.

Key #5

IT MUST IDENTIFY THE RESOURCES YOU WILL NEED

Chances are you will require the assistance of certain people to see your dreams fulfilled. Who are they? How should you approach them? What should you ask them? Is there an association or fellowship you could join? Some goals require the assistance of professional helpers.

Countless thousands have stopped the booze battle with the help of the world-renowned Alcoholics Anonymous 12 Step Program. Key #5 drives us to identify the people, places, organizations and resources necessary to accomplish great things in life. I found there is so much help available for those who stop long enough to consider, shut-up long enough to hear, and humble themselves enough to ask.

Many of the "big guns" in the speaking/training business have freely given of their time to help me. They are delighted to help someone who has the courage to seek assistance and puts into practice the advice given.

Key #6

IT MUST MEET SOME NEED AND INCLUDE BENEFITS

Every goal has a price and requires a certain degree of sacrifice and hard work. When you list the benefits of the goal you stay motivated to stick at it. The question to ask is, "What's in it for me?"

I went to Bermuda four times in 1988 to train sales people for a bank. When I set my 1989 goals, doing more training in Bermuda was high on the list. I cut out pictures of the hotel I stayed at in Hamilton by the harbour. It was such a quiet, and lovely resort. We were right on the water, and could see the cruise lines come in. The smell of the sea air, the warm sunshine, the colourful trees and flowers in that picture got me excited.

I put it right on my computer. Every time I would wonder if I should be working so hard, I would see the hotel and I was mentally transported back to Bermuda and kept on working toward the goal.

This key is an important one. Be sure to list the benefits and consider the emotional advantages. What's in it for me? How will I feel if I accomplish this goal? How will it affect my self-esteem? How will my mind be affected when I reach this goal? Get feelings in the picture. Contemplate the emotional benefits to the goal.

Key #7
IT MUST INCLUDE A WORKABLE PLAN

Time management expert and author Harold Taylor says, "Don't expect to achieve your goals without adequate planning. Planning moves things from where they are now to where we want them to be in the future. It translates intention into action."

Sit down with your daily planner and schedule when you will work on your goals. Make a plan which is realistic given your situation but develop an action plan. List the steps involved and when you will work on them.

Key #8

IT SHOULD HAVE ACCOUNTABILITY FACTORS BUILT IN

Have you tried to achieve a certain goal only to fail time and time again? You feel the goal is worthwhile and you would really like to see it through but you just can't breakthrough. Then perhaps you should consider making yourself accountable to someone you respect.

I have an advisory board who hold me accountable for certain professional goals. I call them my "ATTILA THE HUN COMMITTEE". If I say I will have two chapters of my next book written by the 15th of the month, they ensure I do. I have been massacred at some ATTILA COMMITTEE meetings for not meeting deadlines. They don't let me get away with anything.

This step may seem extreme and it might well be for some goals. But other goals which are essential, can be achieved by using this key, particularly if you have had difficulty with certain parts of the goal.

If a goal is important to you and you need help, find someone who you respect, who is not afraid to confront you and who will honestly hold you to what you agree. You might get together weekly or monthly to review your progress.

One thing we do to help people in our seminars is to have them write out their goals and put them in envelopes we supply. They write their name and address on the envelope. We collect all the sealed envelopes and mail them back to the participants one or two months later. Getting this reminder in the mail is a fantastic way to stay on track with the goals you set out to accomplish.

Accountability is a key which is vital to goal setting success. It may be one of the toughest keys to practice but does it ever produce results.

The California coast was shrouded in fog the morning of July 4th, 1952. Twenty-one miles to the west, on Catalina Island, a 34 year old woman waded into the water and began swimming toward California, determined to be the first woman to ever swim the 21 mile strait. Her name was Florence Chadwick, and she had already been the first woman to swim the English Channel in both

directions. The water was numbingly cold that morning, and the fog was so thick she could hardly see the boats in her own party --there to scare away the sharks. As the hours ticked away, she swam on. Even worse than growing fatigue was the bone-chilling cold of the water.

More than 15 hours later, numbed with the cold, she asked to be taken out. She couldn't go on any longer. Her mother and her trainer, in a boat alongside her, urged her to go on as they were getting close to shore, yet all she could see was dense fog.

A few minutes later, she was taken out of the water, and later, realizing that she had been within a half mile of the shore, blurted out, "I'm not excusing myself, but if I could have seen the shore, I might have made it."

She had been defeated, not really by the cold or even by the fatigue, but by the fog. That thick fog became her focus rather than the shore being her focus. It had blinded her reason and her eyes.

CHAPTER 5

Towards
Spectacular
Self-Confidence

Bill Hybels from South Barrington, Illinois shares the story of two women who are in a personnel office about to be interviewed for the same job. They are both responding to an ad they saw in the local newspaper. They both have children and both are returning to work after being away from the job market for 15 years. Both women want this job.

Lucy sits nervously, fidgeting while she waits for the personnel manager to call her in. Once in the office she sits rigidly, looking very pale, her hands sweating and trembling somewhat. She is breathing shallowly, her heart is racing, she finds it difficult to look the interviewer in the eye.

"Lucy, you have read the ad, you've applied for this job, and you have certain skills. What makes you think you are qualified? In a nutshell, why should I hire you?"

Before she even opens her mouth she has a terrible sinking feeling in the pit of her stomach. She asks herself what she is doing here. Already she feels embarrassed for even having applied for the job. She's ashamed, she feels dejected and flustered. "I guess I was sick of just staying home. I was bored with housework. You see the kids are in school all day and I need something to do. I've cooked some, I've cleaned some." As Lucy mouths those empty words, she is filled with self-doubt and self-hatred. The thought of even trying to enter the competitive job market at her age repulses her. She feels she has blown the interview and leaves the office totally humiliated vowing to never put herself through that type of embarrassment again.

The second woman, Jane, has exactly the same qualifications. She too has been out of the job market for almost 15 years. Her children have grown and her experience is that of a mother and homemaker. She walks into the personnel manager's office with a bounce in her step. She smiles at him, looks him straight in the eye and takes a seat, sitting in a confident posture.

The manager asks her the same question he asked Lucy, "Jane, you have read the ad, you've applied for this job, and you have certain skills. What makes you think you are qualified? In a nutshell, why should I hire you?"

Sitting up straight in her chair she responds by saying, "Mr. Jones I would like you to know a little about me. I've been a housewife for the past 15 years and I think it has made me uniquely qualified to fill this position.

I have personally tutored four children all the way through grammar and grade school. I have done their homework with them and helped them. I know all about new math, new English. I have been a counsellor to my kids in each area of life from college choice to dating.

I am the right person for the job because over the past 15 years I have been a domestic engineer, a purchasing agent, a cook and I have been instrumental in keeping my home intact, which is no easy thing in our day. For the past 15 years I have been:

a meal planner
a nurse
a cop
a judge
a jury
a wardrobe consultant

a budget expert
a financial planner
a teacher
a tutor
a cheer leader
a spiritual adviser
a maid
a linguistic expert
a resident Dear Abby
a gardener
an administrator
a schedule planner
a chauffeur
an environmentalist and
a family traditionalist.

For my husband I have been a friend, a lover, an adviser, an encourager, a partner, a comforter and a constant companion. For my community I have been a caring neighbour, a diligent volunteer, a giving friend and a church member.

Mr. Jones, with that vast amount of experience I have gained an incredible amount of knowledge and skill. Given a little time and training, I am absolutely convinced I can do this job and do it well."

Which one do you think will probably get the job? The facts were almost the same for both women. Why would the outcome be so dramatically different? What did Jane have that Lucy lacked? The answer is self-confidence. One was sure of herself and another doubted herself. If we want to conquer Directional Success-Blockers, we need to remove questions of self-doubt which attempt to sabotage our goal achievements.

Think for a moment of people you consider self-confident. Why do you think they are that way? Where do they appear most confident? How did they get it?

I believe that self-confidence is for everyone, no matter at what income level you find yourself, regardless of your skills or social status. We all have the potential to become self-assured, stable and confident individuals.

Early childhood development

If as a child you had a strong sense of *ACCEPTANCE* from your home environment, chances are you developed well in the area of confidence. You tend to risk more, experience more, if in childhood you felt love and acceptance from your family. If you knew you were of value, no matter what, you had a strong chance of developing well in this area.

Many people are not so fortunate. Some children feel little acceptance at home. They are never certain if they are loved or not. In some homes the bottom line is, "I'll show you love if you measure up to my expectations... If not, tough luck". Love is always conditional.

Also important is the *APPROVAL* factor. People who are naturally self-confident grow up with a lot of verbal affirmations. Their parents would never scream at them the way some parents do - even in public. Instead they are affirmed and acknowledged for trying hard. They are told often how important they were and how much they were appreciated.

The third ingredient from childhood which affects our self-confidence level is the *AFFECTION* we receive. Was it a common practice in your home to be hugged and kissed? Were you held and nurtured? Did you hear how special and precious you were? If so, you probably had a strong sense of internal surety.

People who don't get this input, are often obsessed with them in later years. They lack acceptance so they clamour like crazy to fit in or belong somewhere. Without approval they are addicted to convincing everyone that they matter. Similarly, without childhood experience of affection, people often grow up to behave in a way that demands affection from others. What they really want is for someone to scream, "I love you, I love you."

An unknown author has written these powerful thoughts, expressing the influence for good or evil that our lives exert on others. After reading each statement, ask yourself, "Are people learning this from me?"

If a child lives with criticism, he learns to condemn.

If a child lives with hostility, he learns to fight.

If a child lives with fear, he learns to be apprehensive.

If a child lives with pity, he learns to feel sorry for himself.

If a child lives with jealousy, he learns to feel guilty.

If a child lives with encouragement, he learns to be
self-confident.

If a child lives with tolerance, he learns to be patient.

If a child lives with praise, he learns to be appreciative.

If a child lives with acceptance, he learns to love.

If a child lives with approval, he learns to like himself.

If a child lives with recognition, he learns to have a goal.

If a child lives with fairness, he learns what justice is.

If a child lives with honesty, he learns what truth is.

If a child lives with sincerity he learns to have faith in himself
and those around him.

If a child lives with love, he learns that the world is a
wonderful place to live in.

Self-esteem and self-confidence are similar but they are concerned with two very different things. Self-esteem attempts to answer the question, "Do I matter?" and self-confidence deals with "Do I have skills?" The latter is concerned with ability and the former with worth.

The following are necessary ingredients to developing healthy self-confidence.

SECURITY

We all need to know that our relationships with others and even to some extent with ourselves are secure and free from being tied to performance.

By that, if I am to develop self-confidence, I need to know that pass or fail, relationships will still be there. I need to be convinced that sink or swim I am a valuable individual.

Like a child who's not sure that his parents will love him if he fails, I too will not risk losing that love. I need that security and without it I will never risk. Security is too important!

OPPORTUNITY

Self-confidence is concerned with ability. A necessary ingredient therefore in this area is opportunity to prove and test my abilities.

What area of your life would you consider yourself fairly self-confident in? Would you say you have had a recent positive experience in that area? Sure, we are confident in the areas we do well in. If we win certain battles we are confident in facing others. It's like the marine officer, when he saw that he and his men were surrounded by the enemy, said, "Men, we are surrounded on all sides; don't let one of them get away." We have certain abilities and we can test them out in the forum of life.

ACKNOWLEDGEMENT

In order for us to grow into self-confident individuals we need the acknowledgement which says, "You are super! That was fantastic. You matter. You did a great job."

We all need to be reminded that we are special. We need it from others and from ourselves.

Want More Self-confidence?

1. SPECIFY YOUR COMPETENCIES

What are you competent at? What are some things you do fairly well. There is no such answer as, "Nothing" to that question. I refuse to accept that and so should you. It is a blatant lie to answer that question by saying, "Who me? I can't do anything well". That's baloney. Look a little deeper.

We all have certain strengths and abilities whether in knowledge, character, past experiences or personality traits. Specify what you are good at. Repeat those things to yourself and start doing more of those things which are positive for you.

DO YOU HAVE ANY OF THE FOLLOWING QUALITIES?

Care about others	Detail orientated
Good with numbers	Strong willed
Wood working skills	Good cook
Sing well	Creative
Listen to others	Good swimmer
Organizer	Write poetry
Dances	Fast typist
Know 2 languages	Can give a speech
Can drive a truck	Know CPR
Has a hobby	Good at a game
Enjoys hunting or fishing	Knowledgeable about history
Memorize verses easily	Play a musical instrument
Crafty	Sew well
Handy man	Travel experience
Love people	Love for animals
Know someone famous	Have an interesting collection
Works diligently	Cares about integrity
Honest	Sense of humour

2. STRETCH YOUR COMPETENCIES

Self-confidence is nothing more than knowledge. Let me say that again. To be self-confident all you need is information. Look at it this way. You do something well, five thousand times. You know you can do it. If you've done it right that many times, you know you can do it therefore you are confident. If you have never done it before you don't KNOW.

Without that knowledge you doubt. If you want to be confident then give yourself the chance to find out what your abilities are. By trying new things and taking the risk to stretch your present level of ability, you discover that trying is the key. You come to know that taking a chance is not the end of the world. You realize that security and peace are not the grounds on which self-confidence are developed. Without at least trying you know you are living well below your ability level.

Self-doubt is a progressive illness. When you refuse to risk and try confidence building projects you begin the downward spiral of rejecting growth opportunities and settling instead for the safety net of life.

That pattern is the "safety net" syndrome. You refuse to leave the nest, you don't try anything that in anyway threatens the security and safety factors.

When was the last time you tried something you've never done before?

When were you last exposed to some growth opportunity? By taking some risk and succeeding you create that pattern of stretching your ability and increasing your knowledge about your skill level. What kind of a risk-taker are you?

DECISION MAKING STYLE

Think of the important life decisions you have made and then answer the following questions. You may not answer some with complete confidence, but give the answers that come closest to what you believe.

This is not a test; it is just a device to help you understand your own decision-making style. For each dimension, choose the one response out of three that best describes how you usually respond in making big decisions.

I. Anxiety Factor

1. In thinking about making a risky decision, I feel mostly anxiety.
2. In thinking about making a risky decision, I feel a mixture of fear and excitement.
3. I am mostly excited when having to make risky decisions.

II. Information Factor

1. I will consider new information even after I've arrived at a probable decision.
2. I don't want to hear new information after I've made up my mind.
3. I feel compelled either to seek out new information or to shut it out after I've made a probable decision.

III. Speed Factor

1. I usually make decisions - even big ones - quickly.
2. I take a considerable amount of time to make big decisions.
3. I usually take a very long time with considerable thought before making a big decision.

IV. Change Factor

1. I prefer safety to risk.
2. I value safety and risk about equally.
3. I prefer risk to safety.

V. Emotional Factor

1. I decide by reasoning and take my feelings into account.
2. I rely almost exclusively on feelings.
3. I completely discount feelings and emotion.

VI. Choice Factor

1. I make a quick overall survey of possibilities hoping that something will hit me.
2. I keep producing ideas and then going over my possible choices.
3. I think of alternatives but stop after a reasonable search.

VII. Right Factor

1. I believe there is one right decision, and it is my job to uncover it.
2. I believe there is no one right decision; I just need to find one that is good enough.
3. I believe in choosing the first decision that really hits me.

VIII. Outcome Factor

1. I don't try to predict the outcome of decisions because I expect things will work out the way I intend.
2. I focus in on all the possibilities that might go wrong.
3. I think of both the good and the bad outcomes of my decisions.

IX. Decision Factor

1. Once decided, I usually don't think about it again.
2. Once I've made up my mind, I often experience serious doubts and often change my mind.
3. Once I've decided, I usually rally behind it after rechecking.

X. What If Factor

1. After deciding, I tend to worry or regret the decision.
2. After deciding, I tend to put it out of my mind.
3. After deciding, I usually am secure but review the facts.

Scoring Instructions

1. Circle the number you picked for each question, on the list below.
2. We have given each number a letter. Count all the A's, B's, and C's .
3. Write the total number of A's, B's, C's etc.
4. Whichever letter was circled the most is your style according to the three categories below.

QUESTIONS	ANSWERS		
I.	1. A	2. B	3. C
II.	1. B	2. C	3. A
III.	1. C	2. B	3. A
IV.	1. A	2. B	3. C
V.	1. B	2. C	3. A
VI.	1. C	2. A	3. B
VII.	1. A	2. B	3. C
VIII.	1. C	2. A	3. B
IX.	1. C	2. A	3. B
X.	1. A	2. C	3. B

Totals: A's ____ B's____ C's____

If A was the most common letter circled, you are a...

● **CAUTIOUS RISK TAKER**

The Cautious Risk Taker makes big decisions with great effort and anxiety. They are afraid of making mistakes, take a lot of time, and tend to worry about the consequences of their decisions.

If B was the most common letter circled, you are a...

● **BALANCED RISK TAKER**

The Balanced Risk Taker makes decisions fairly slowly. They tend to be more concerned with outcomes than with failure. They need to make a good decision, and tend to plan and review but without worrying too much.

If C was the most common letter circled, you are an...

● **ADVENTUROUS RISK TAKER**

The adventurous risk taker is rather careless. They make big decisions quickly with little experience of mixed feeling. They can be classified as inappropriately optimistic. They waste little time in retrospective or evaluative thought.

Confidence comes through a series of success experiences. You do something well, you increase your knowledge, you try it again and the pattern is set.

3. GET HELP IF NEEDED

Some people feel a need to cover up a lack of self-confidence by trying to make a big impression. A newly promoted Army colonel moved into his new and impressive office. As he sat behind his new big desk, a private knocked at his door. "Just a minute," the colonel said, "I'm on the phone."

He picked up the receiver and said loudly, "Yes, sir General. I'll call the President this afternoon. No sir, I won't forget." Then he hung up the phone and told the private to come in. "What can I help you with?" "Well, sir," the private replied,

"I've come to hook up that phone."

There is help available to assist in giving you some positive success experience. People who fear public speaking have become confident speakers by joining a Toastmasters Club. They provide the platform and opportunity to stretch your competencies.

If you want to get more self-confidence you should join Toastmasters International. The cost is peanuts compared to the immense value of the organization. To find a club in your area, look in the telephone book or contact them at Toastmasters International, P.O. Box 9052, Mission Viejo, California, 92690-7052, Telephone: (714) 858-8255. Toastmasters is only one organization dedicated to helping develop your self-confidence. There are thousands. Find one that's right for you.

Don't be so proud that you can't ask for help. Refuse to be like the man who said, " I by my stupidity got into this mess; therefore I by my stupidity will get out."

Be careful of the "If Only" syndrome. What this 'excuse-giving' syndrome does is attempt to put off self-development by coming up with reasons to delay.

"If only I had a boyfriend..."

"If only I had more money..."

"If only I was more attractive..."

"If only I had less stress/more friends/less hassles/more creativity/less inflation/more breaks in life..."

Self-Confidence Tips

- Join a status building association, club or organization
- Meet some important people
- Buy an expensive suit
- Do something you are good at 25 times in the next month
- Write out and repeat self-confidence building affirmations
- Spend time with confident people

- Refuse to host or attend any "Pity Parties"
- Hold your body as a confident person would
- Remove anything in your life which contributes to self-doubt
- Take a risk
- Get on a talk-show
- Start verbalizing that you are a confident person
- Concentrate on what's right with you
- Make a list of all your victories, successes and achievements
- Free yourself from addictions
- Act confidently
- Increase your vocabulary
- Develop an expertise in something
- Get good at a hobby
- Take up something unique
- Read up on an subject that interests your boss
- Set a small goal and achieve it
- Help someone less fortunate
- Take a risk
- Create a Hit List of influential people you want to meet
- Buy a book on communication
- Listen to powerful audio cassettes
- Speak up
- Give a speech
- Take an adventurous trip
- Take a Self-Defense course
- Attend a Self-esteem seminar

I created the list below and ad to it frequently. I call it my "Hit list" of people I would like to meet. I check off once I have met the person. What a confidence builder to meet powerful people!

MY PARTIAL "HIT LIST"

YOU WILL HELP ME MEET THESE PEOPLE!

Billy Graham	James Taylor	Chuck Swindoll
Sandi Patti	James Dobson	Og Mandino
Zig Ziglar ‡	Peter Uberoth	Dr. Norman Vincent Peale ‡
Jim Janz ‡	Rich DeVos	Mother Theresa
Prince Charles	George Bush	Ronald Reagan
Jimmy Carter	Richard Nixon	Gerald Ford
Bill Bright ‡	Phil Donahue	Frank Abagnale
Cavett Robert ‡	Connie Chung	Tom Peters ‡
Jesse Jackson	Peter Hansen ‡	Michael Jackson
Paul McCartney	George Harrison	Ringo Starr
Sammy Davis Jr.	Denis Waitley ‡	Pete Rose
Kevin Dyer	Gerry Gilles	Jay Leno
B.J. Thomas	Johnny Carson	Sally Jessy Raphael
Donald Trump	Armand Hammer	Stevie Wonder
Harvey MacKay	Wayne Gretzy	Hulk Hogan
Mayor Cain	Mr. T	Diane Sawyer
Chuck Norris	John Denver	Wayne Newton
Mary Kay Ash	Betty Ford	Tony Robbins ‡
Tom Sullivan	Leo Buscaglia	Scott Peck
John Bradshaw	Tom Winninger ‡	Bette Midler
Carol Burnett	Barbara Walters	Dr. Robert H. Schuller ‡
Mike Warnke	Joel Weldon	Anne Gillian
Nancy Reagan	Nelson Mandela	Kenneth Blanchard ‡
Dan Rather	Oprah Winphrey	Margaret Thatcher
Rich Little	Jerry Falwell	Joni Erickson-Tada
Peter Lowe ‡	Lee Iaccoca	Mark Victor Hansen ‡

‡ I have already met these people. This works!

Be a strong person. Develop a sense of destiny. Know who you are and what you are about. Be proud of who you are and what you will accomplish in this life. When others sense you have a strong self-confidence and healthy self-esteem they will be willing to believe in you, trust and follow you. We are all attracted to dynamic leaders. In the next chapter, you will read about 10 practical ways you can become a leader others would be delighted to support and work for.

CHAPTER 6

BE A LEADER OTHERS CAN FOLLOW
10 Ways to Make Others Believe in You

"One of the most universal cravings of our time is a hunger
for compelling and creative leadership."

James McGregor Burns

People are not leaders by virtue of their position. No, real
leadership involves much more. You might be the "boss", might
have "President or Manager" on your business card but that does
not make you a leader. Leadership involves the ability to lead. A
leader is someone who knows where he/she is going and is able to
persuade others to go along.

An organization short on money can borrow and one with
poor facilities can build but if its short on leadership it has little
prospect for survival.

10 WAYS
TO MAKE OTHERS BELIEVE IN YOU

1. DEVELOP STRONG PERSONAL CONVICTIONS

People are more convinced by the depth of your convictions than by the height of your logic. Be a person who has causes and convictions. We live in a day where leaders seem to waiver a whole lot as to where they stand. Politicians seem to respond to whatever others would want to hear. What's really important to you? Stick with those things. Be clear as to your place in life. Know what you want out of life and where you see your ship sailing to. Practice consistency.

Two rules to avoid:

> ## Rule #1 The boss is always right!
> ## Rule #2 When the boss is wrong refer to Rule #1!

2. BECOME HIGHLY INFECTIOUS!

Leaders have developed inner qualities that attract others to themselves. Here are a few of such characteristics:

Self Starters

Leaders who attract others are known for their ability to take initiative. They don't wait for the committee or wait to be asked to get the job done. They can get their fires burning without depending on external stimuli.

Honesty

The fastest way to repulse people and lose friends is to be anything less than painstakingly honest. The surest way to ruin credibility is to tell "white lies". People will not tolerate a person who compromises this point.

Humility

Humility is that sense of strength that says to others, "I am not the be all and end all of life. I am willing to have an open mind, to listen to ideas." The last person I want to be around is the person who is so full of himself. Billy Graham once said , "the smallest package in the world is a man all wrapped up in himself."

Fairness

Fairness will endear others to you. When position and responsibility allow us to pass judgement, we must practice fairness, not favouritism if we want to attract others.

Emotional Control

There is nothing wrong with blowing off steam once in a while. It's the loss of control that ruins the impact of many potential great leaders. The concern here is management of emotion, not avoidance or denial, but control. Very few leaders are free from criticism. Their control and humility will nowhere be seen more clearly than in the manner they accept and react to scrutiny.

Humour

There are experts like Neil Muscot and Steve Donohue who making a considerable income just teaching people how to lighten up. Humour attracts people, provided it is suitable, clean and not a put-down type humour. Life is short and making others laugh a little is a definite asset.

Positive Attitude

People are attracted to positive people. Who wants to follow a sour-puss? Not me! Instead in a dark and negative world ,the positive leader shines and draws others to him/herself.

Flexibility

A bumper sticker read, "Be reasonable - just do it my way!" Will that attitude draw or repulse people? Would you commit yourself to a leader who refuses to consider any way other than their own? Strong leaders are versatile. They can be highly resourceful by adapting to the style of others.

3. SUBORDINATE YOUR LIFE UNDER YOUR GOALS

We have already considered the issue of goal setting. It bears repeating somewhat again under the topic of leadership. Leaders who have a high degree of credibility live their lives under the guidelines of their goals. They have direction and focus. As we consider becoming greater leaders perhaps now is the time to look at submitting our lives to our goals from another angle.

Subordinating your life under your goals says:

● I know want I to accomplish. I will get there!

● I have evaluated my strengths and weaknesses and these goals will benefit everyone. They are fair goals.

● I am on a track and you will notice consistency and congruency in everything I do.

● I am committed to issues, to visions, to causes.

● I believe in myself, my destiny, my work, to set goals and submit myself to their constraints. I will not waiver, I know what I want and where I am headed.

4. WELCOME CHANGE

"January 31, 1829

To: President Jackson

The canal system of this country is being threatened by the spread of a new form of transportation known as "railroads." The federal government must preserve the canals for the following reasons:

One. If canal boats are supplanted by "railroads," serious unemployment will result. Captains, cooks, drivers, hostlers, repairmen and lock tenders will be left without means of livelihood, not to mention the numerous farmers now employed in growing hay for horses.

Two. Boat builders would suffer and towline whip and harness makers would be left destitute.

Three. Canal boats are absolutely essential to the defense of the United States. In the event of the expected trouble with England, the Erie Canal would be the only means by which we could ever move the supplies so vital to waging modern war.

As you may well know, Mr. President,"railroad" carriages are pulled at the enormous speed of 15 miles per hour by "engines" which, in addition to endangering life and limb of passengers, roar and snort their way through the countryside, setting fire to crops, scaring the livestock and frightening women and children. The Almighty certainly never intended that people should travel at such breakneck speed.

> Signed, Martin Van buren
> Governor of New York

Often our early resistance to change seems rather foolish with a slightly different perspective. People will not follow a sniffling wimp. People are not recruited to a job but a cause. Leaders who attract the greatest quality and quantity of people are deeply committed to some great cause. They have a sense of mission.

Sales trainer Tom Stoyan, says, "You must have passion to succeed". It's true. Leaders must attract others by conveying a sense of purpose and significance to what they are being called to.

5. SEE THE POTENTIAL IN OTHERS

- Great minds discuss Ideas
- Average minds discuss Events
- Small minds discuss People

Never see someone for where they are today but for where they can go. Within each person is a vast amount of untapped potential. Leaders look beyond the outer appearance to the inner development possibilities. Go out of your way to find the best in others and you will have more people to lead than you will ever need. Look beyond the impatience to see the potential calm. Look beyond the awkwardness of present social behaviour. See not the cocoon but the butterfly. See not the rough stone but the polished diamond.

John Masefield wrote of Churchill:

"This man in darkness saw

In doubting led

in danger did

In utter most despair showed hope

that made the midnight fair

The world he saved, calls blessings on his head.

This man in darkness, saw."

6. GET STRONG COME DECISION TIME

Strong leaders can make strong decisions and live by them. They don't shun responsibility. President Jimmy Carter is one such individual. On April 25, 1980, 50 American hostages had been in captivity for 173 days. The President of the United States appeared on television to disclose the failed military attempt to rescue the hostages. After President Carter described the events which led to the aborted mission, he stated, "It was my decision to attempt the rescue operation. It was my decision to cancel it when problems developed. The responsibility is fully my own."

Decision making undoubtedly is one of the most critical of all leadership functions. It can make or break a leader almost immediately. It requires tremendous internal courage. Lack of courage in this area has been the downfall of many otherwise good leaders. There is nothing more frustrating for subordinates than having to deal with a weak-minded leadership who refuse to be decisive.

Excuses are not the fare of good leadership. All of us are tempted to make rather ridiculous excuses to others. If we would consciously examine our excuses, we would discover how ridiculous most of them sound. Someone has collected a few choice excuses that were offered in relation to automobile accidents:

- "An invisible car came out of nowhere, struck my car and vanished."
- "I had been driving my car for 40 years when I fell asleep at the wheel and had the accident."
- "I pulled away from the side of the road, lunged at my mother-in-law, and headed over the embankment."
- "The pedestrian had no idea which direction to go, so I ran over him."

7. SOLICIT STRONG COMMITMENT

Leaders have to sell ideas, concepts and roles. How do you motivate others? Sell motives. A motive is something within that excites. There is extrinsic motivation which comes from without. Money, awards and recognition are all extrinsic motivators. Intrinsic motivators are another type, and they are far more effective because they come from within. Inner motivation can give a sense of worth to an individual or inspire commitment to a worthy cause.

The communist party, despite its current collapse throughout Europe, accomplished a phenomenal portion of its goals in under 50 years. The communists set a goal to dominate the world with communism in less than 50 years and have succeeded at one third of their goal. That is impressive. They solicited a strong commitment from their members. Douglas Hyde's book, <u>Leadership and Dedication</u>, describes how much commitment they got from people because they asked for it. Granted, they used this principle in ways which I disagree with, but Hyde's observation is that if you demand little from others that's what you'll get. Place strong demands on the people you lead and they will be willing to follow and give much. The test of a great leader is not what he does, but what others do as a result of what he does.

8. DEVELOP PEOPLE SKILLS

As you get better at relating to others, they will allow you to get close to them. Once they allow you to get close you have a greater chance to influence them. But you have to get close first.

People skills includes:

- Acknowledging others.
- Affirming others.
- Praising others.
- Recognizing the effort of others.
- Conveying warmth to others.
- Caring enough to confront others.
- Being transparent with others.
- Developing listening skills.
- Building others up.
- Talking positively about people to others.
- Looking people in the eye.
- Conveying "I care about you" with your body language.
- Calling people back immediately.
- Never interrupting people.

- Matching and mirroring the behaviourof others.
- Sending PHN's. (Personal Handwritten Notes)
- Keeping track of important dates and respond with calls, card and gifts.
- Never using put-down humour.
- Showing genuine interest in the whole person.
- Clearing up misunderstandings and conflicts quickly.

"You do not lead by
hitting people over the head -- that's assault,
not leadership."

Einstein

---

9. LEARN TO COMMUNICATE

There is nothing quite so wonderful as a good idea; there is nothing so tragic as a good idea which cannot be communicated. The effectiveness of your leadership potential is directly related to your ability to communicate. Individuals who can verbalize their ideas, dreams and concepts - so they are heard, understood and acted upon - possess one of the primary qualities of solid leadership.

The greatest leaders are great communicators. How are you in this area? Are you understood? Have you ever taken a course or seminar on effective communication? Perhaps a book could help if you need to develop in this area. One of the most remarkable men I know is Vince Robert, my uncle. This super positive thinker became convinced in later life of the importance of communication. He had a successful taxi cab company but he could not read or write. He knew that to be truly alive, he would need to remove the barriers he had to communication.

He learned to read and write by placing a huge family size dictionary on the front seat of his taxi cab. Between calls he read, studied and memorized words and their meanings. He still has that dictionary and believe me, it is well worn. It should be enshrined in the Successiblity Thinker's Hall of Fame. Here's a man dedicated to leadership and development. He has impacted this world in a big way because of his strength and determination. His office holds several hundred books which he has, of course, read from cover to cover. What an inspiration!

EXAMPLE OF MISCOMMUNICATION

A woman went to a lawyer and said she wanted a divorce. The lawyer got out his note pad, and proceeded to ask her some questions.

"Do you have any grounds?"

"Oh, yes," she replied. "About three quarters of an acre."

The lawyer paused for a moment, then proceeded. "Do you have a grudge?"

"No," the woman answered quickly. "But we do have a lovely carport." Again the lawyer paused and then asked, "Does he beat you up?"

"No. I get up before he does every morning," the woman reported.

Finally the lawyer blurted, "Lady, why do you want to divorce your husband?"

"It's because," she exclaimed, "that man can't carry on an intelligent conversation."

Brent Barlow in Salt
Lake City,
Deseret News

COMMUNICATION SECRETS OF GREAT LEADERS

Clue #1   To have spoken does not mean I have been heard.

Clue #2   To touch people I need to develop transparency.

Clue #3   There must be consistency in what I say and what
                 others see me do.

Clue #4   Feedback helps me be sure I am understood.

Clue #5   Asking questions is better than making statements.

Clue #6   Uncover how others are perceiving you by asking
                 questions.

Clue #7   Give others the time they need to say what they have
                 to say.

Clue #8   Never be more than half an inch more enthusiastic
                 than others.

Clue #9   Match the voice qualities of the people you
                 communicate with. Voice qualities include pace,
                 volume, pitch.

Clue #10   Better to say little and have someone think you an
                 idiot than to say too much and remove all doubt.

A man was walking down a residential street and noticed a man struggling with a washing machine at the doorway of his house. When he volunteered to help, the homeowner was overjoyed and the two men together began to work and struggle with the bulky appliance. After several minutes of fruitless effort the two stopped and just looked at each other. They looked as if they were on the verge of total exhaustion. Finally, when they caught their breath, the first man said to the homeowner:"We'll never get this washing machine in there!" To which the homeowner replied: "In! I'm trying to move it out of here!!!"

How many leadership problems are due to faulty communications? How many marriages crash on the rocks because people don't know how to communicate? How many teenagers leave home because of ineffective communication skills? The need is obvious - Leaders are communicators.

10. DEVELOP A SERVANT'S HEART

> "The measure of a man is not how many servants
> he has, but how many men he serves."
>
> Moody

Now here's a concept that won't go over well with a lot of readers! "What are you talking about? I'm in-charge now, I have worked hard to get here. If I show weakness I'm cooked."

This type of leader works hard to control others and loves to shout out commands from "on high". They may be in-charge but they are far from being a leader others will want to follow. A servant puts aside his own needs, wants and priorities to give to the people he serves. To be the leader of many you must be the servant of many. There is no limit to the good that a man can do, if he doesn't care who gets the credit.

This, I am fully aware goes against the thinking of many today. Go into any organization where the organizational chart is displayed and you will see that the leader has his name at the top with lines running from top to bottom.

A story is told of a military patrol recovering enemy territory. Everyone was taut as piano strings. Suddenly the point soldier was mortally wounded. The Sergeant screamed for the unit to take cover. A young soldier rushed to his fallen buddy and was wounded himself. In great pain he dragged the now dead solder back. The Sergeant asked him why he got himself shot. He answered, "Sarge, I had to hear him say, ' I knew you'd come.'" That's commitment.

What I am espousing is something which could be called the Jesus Leadership Concept. Regardless of what you think of this Jesus figure, he did have a leadership impact on this world. One of the things he said was, "If one of you wants to be great, he must be the servant of the rest;" Talk about revolutionary thinking. Look at what he accomplished. He taught that to lead you had to serve. The way up is down.

This is not to say you let the sheep lead the shepherds. Not at all. It's an attitude of service. C.H. Spurgeon said, "It needs more skill than I can tell to play the second fiddle well." Someone else has said, "The branch that bears the most fruit is bent the lowest to the ground."

"The true way to be humble is not to stoop until you are smaller than yourself, but to stand at your real height against some higher nature that will show you what the real smallness of your greatness is." Phillips Brooks

MANAGEMENT VS LEADERSHIP

Do we want to be managed? No way. We want to be led. Whoever heard of a world manager? World leader, yes. Educational leader. Political leader. Religious leader. Scout leader. Community leader. Labour leader. Business leader. They lead. They don't manage. You can lead your horse to water, but you can't manage him to drink. If you want to manage somebody, manage yourself. Once you have succeeded here then you are ready to lead others.

LIFE

They told me that Life could be just what I made it --
Life could be fashioned and worn like a gown;
I, the designer; mine the decision
Whether to wear it with bonnet or crown.

And so I selected the prettiest pattern --
Life should be made of the rosiest hue --
Something unique, and a bit out of fashion,
One that perhaps would be chosen by few.

But other folks came and they leaned o'er my shoulder;
Somebody questioned the ultimate cost;
Somebody tangled the thread I was using;
One day I found that my scissors were lost.

And somebody claimed the material faded;
Somebody said I'd be tired ere 'twas worn;
Somebody's fingers, too pointed and spiteful,
Snatched at the cloth, and I saw it was torn.

Oh! somebody tried to do all the sewing,
Wanting always to advise or condone.
Here is my life, the product of many;
Where is that gown I could fashion -- alone?

Nan Terrell Reed

---◆---

CONQUERING THE OPERATIONAL SUCCESS-BLOCKERS

---◆---

CHAPTER 7

ESCAPE
THE TYRANNY
OF THE URGENT:
10 Ways
To Save Time

Are you juggling more tasks than ever but getting less done? Do you ever wish there was thirty hours in a day? Could you use a little extra time? Do you leave a trail of unfinished jobs? Any letters unanswered? Unvisited friends? Unpurchased gifts? Is your life harried? Need relief?

If you are anything like me, and I suspect you are, you need to conquer and remove the Operational Success-Blockers of life. These Success-Blockers are the obstacles that take us off track on a daily basis. You can be motivated, have a fantastic attitude with all kinds of enthusiasm, you can have conquered the Directional Success-Blockers so you know exactly what you want out of life, but if you lose it here on the operation side of things, you will never leave the starting gate.

IT'S ABOUT TIME!

How many of the following statements reflect your current belief about time?

- I should follow the plan I have for the day at all costs.
- I am severely overworked.
- I never feel there is enough time to accomplish what's really important.
- Given my schedule, it's impossible for me to perform on the basis of priorities.
- I work better under pressure.
- I enjoy the freedom to procrastinate
- I don't always know where to start the big jobs I have to do.
- If I had more time I would get more done.
- People hamper my productivity.
- I need to get more sleep if I am to be at top performance.
- I can't schedule uninterrupted time in my daily planner.
- I could never stop procrastinating.
- My job is too unpredictable to plan my activities.
- It's better to do the small jobs first and save the demanding ones for the end of the day.
- I can't control my time.
- I am at the mercy of others.
- The telephone wastes a lot of my time.
- Interruptions are out of my control.
- Paper is a hindrance and does little other than clutter my life.
- I waste a fair amount of time struggling with habits I should have broken ages ago.
- I am under a tremendous amount of pressure.
- I waste hours in non-productive activities.
- I often do the urgent at the expense of the important.
- I lose time dealing with mail.

This chapter deals with the management of time. It will provide practical methods you can use to get more done in less time. It will also provide you with tools to control time in a more effective manner if you happened to have identified with more than 4 statements in the above list.

Before I share the 10 ways to save time, let me first challenge some of your notions about time. Take for example, the idea that you work better under pressure. Do you really work "better" or do you just work "faster"? If you are in the regular habit of waiting until the last minute to start major projects, you are likely to produce slip-shod quality, something less than you know you are capable of producing.

Take the assumption that there is never enough time to do all that needs to get done. The truth is, there is always enough time to get done what is essential. What you may need some help in, is deciding the priority of each item. We will cover that later. You may believe that you are too busy to plan activities. Well, perhaps you should change your thinking to, "The busier I get, the more important it is for me to plan."

Are you really overworked? You may be, but could it simply be a case of needing to learn say "No" more often or learning how to delegate? Are interruptions really outside of your control? If I told you, "I'll give you a million dollars if you cut low priority interruptions in half during high priority tasks", do you think you could limit the time you spend dealing with low priority interruptions in your life. It's not we can't, it's more we don't or even won't.

KEY QUESTIONS

1. Is it worth doing at all?
2. Should someone else do it?
3. Should it be done now?
4. To what extent should it be done?
5. Should something else be done?

6. Has someone else already done it?
7. Is it consistent with my objectives?
8. What is urgent and what is important in this task?
9. What part of it can be omitted?
10. Will it make a big difference in the long run?

We all have the same amount of time to deal with everyday. Nothing more, nothing less. Drucker points out, that effective time managers spend their time not merely doing things right but doing the right things. This chapter will cover the 10 ways to save time.

It includes...

- Controlling Bad Habits
- Identifying Pressure
- Identifying The Minute-Taker Wasters
- Identifying Priorities Quickly
- Controlling Procrastination
- Re-thinking Interruptions
- Getting The Most From Your Daily Planner
- Freeing Your Mind (B.F. System)
- Tackling The Telephone
- Implementing Time Savers

"Habit is a cable;
we weave a thread of it every day,
and at last we cannot break it."

Horace Mann

1. CONTROLLING BAD HABITS

That statement is both true and false. True in the sense that before we know it something which we thought we could easily master or control is now much more difficult. It is a false statement because I do not believe any habit is unbreakable. Every habit can be subjected to our control. Controlling bad habits leads the list for ways to save time. This is where we begin in the process of conquering the Operational Success-Blockers. It is the foundation upon which we build solid time management structures. Therefore before the discussion of time saving tips we need to develop the skill of controlling our habits.

Show me any person with a strong sense of self-control and I'll show you a winner. Conversely a loser has little control. So whatever will come in the subsequent sections of this book is immaterial unless we develop the ability to change those habits which hamper our success.

What makes Gretzy such a superstar? Why do some sales people earn ten times what other salespeople earn selling exactly the same product in the same company? Do they have ten times the skill? Hardly. Could they see ten times the prospects? No. Do they have ten times the intelligence, training or drive? No, they have control of their habits and developed the essence of self-control.

The really high achievers in life have a common denominator - they have mastered their habits. Take a look for a minute at the really poor achievers in life; the opposite is true of them. The under achievers have failed miserably because they lack self-discipline. They always let things slip. They seem to have not given enough attention and concern for the important things in life. These people seem to have chosen the path of least resistance. They tried to take the easy way out because it meant less work on the hard things in life, namely change and control - me! Who are the most productive and successful people you know? Would they be characterized as people who have mastered habits? Are they highly disciplined people? How many people do you really know who you would give the label - "Highly disciplined"? Can you name ten? Five? Two?

THE SECRET OF CONTROLLING HABITS

DELAYED   GRATIFICATION

Delayed gratification can be defined as the delaying of the reward or pleasure phase and counting on, even scheduling of the investment or problem phase first in order to more fully enjoy the benefits later. It's getting the unpleasant task done first to enjoy the gratification more deeply later.

How far would Wayne Gretzy get if he tried to put the blessing or victory phase before the "work-out" or investment phase? When the game came he wouldn't last without the early morning runs and late night practices. There's no way he could handle the game without delaying certain pleasures in order to more fully enjoy the victory phase later.

Delayed Gratification means working on problems NOW. It may be tough, sure it will be stretching. But you agree that for you to really enjoy the pleasure or pay-off phase you will work hard first. You forgo now so you can reap more later.

HOW TO PRACTICE SELF-DISCIPLINE

ADVANCED DECISION MAKING

Advanced decision making is the most powerful way to get any habit under control. This involves asking yourself some tough questions on how you will practice this thing called self-discipline. The answer is by making decisions in advance about how you will conduct the affairs of your life.

Let me share with you how I put this idea to practice in my life. My family has a history of early death. People in my family tree have a history of checking out at a young age. The two main causes are heart disease and alcoholism.

My father died at 54 from alcoholism, my older brother Ivan, died at 27 from virtually the same illness. I have several uncles and aunts who have died from heart failure. My sister had a heart attack at 33 years of age. I decided that those two options didn't really turn me on. I know that if I'm going to succeed in my goal of not dying an early death from a heart that stops pumping or a liver that stops functioning because it's pickled in booze, I need to take a few steps. For me those steps involve planning on the pain period first. It involves exercising regularly, weight control and as far as the alcoholism issue, not drinking. I am willing to subject myself to that to reach the goal of living better and longer. I am delaying the gratification those things would bring in order to live longer.

Now comes Advanced Decision Making. I made a decision to not drink. You see I'm a smart guy. I figured out, if I don't drink there is no way I'm gonna die from alcoholism. Pretty smart, eh! I decide in advance - DO NOT DRINK.

So when well intentioned friends come to me on a hot day in August while I'm beside the pool and offer me a real cool beer, there is not even a question in my mind. The answer is No.

In my case, that door is shut, based on a decision I made in advance. If I waited to decide every time I am offered - I would drink. The same applies when I am upset and want to drink or when I feel depressed. I simply don't listen to that little voice inside my head that says "Go have a shot of whisky, it will relax you. It will make things better."

Advanced Decision Making says: "It's already been decided. I live my life based on decisions made in advance. The decision cannot, will not be reversed."

Wayne Gretzy did not decide every morning if he "felt" like practising. No way. He got up to practice every morning at 4 and 5 a.m. because he had decided in advance that if he was to become the world's greatest hockey player he would have to practice.

He got up because he thought the investment was worth it. He did not wait to see if he felt like practising. When the alarm went off, he got up because that's what he (and his dad) decided in advance he would do.

THREE LIES OF THE HABIT DEMONS

Every time a person breaks a commitment and falls back into a bad habit they have bought into one of the three lies of the Habit Demons.

Think back when you started a bad habit again or think about what happens to every alcoholic who falls off the wagon or a person who gains back the weight they lost or someone who wastes piles of time dealing with issues they once had under control. These three lies rear their ugly heads, we buy into them, then fall.

LIE #1
"ONCE WILL BE ENOUGH"

"Just have one beer, one smoke, one dessert." Anytime you hear something inside that sounds like this it's lie #1. Is one beer enough for an alcoholic? No, one is too many and a thousand is not enough. Whenever you hear, "once" or "just this time" let a red flag remind you about the Habit Demons' lies.

LIE #2
"MESS IT UP GOOD"

Once you give in to Lie #1 and do something you know you shouldn't, then Lie #2 kicks in. "Now that you've blown it, mess it up good." It looks like this for someone trying to control the bad habit of eating late at night. "Just have one piece of pie. One little piece can't hurt you. You deserve just one small piece." So you start cutting yourself a piece. Soon afterwards you hear Lie #2. "Well, now you've done it. You might as well have another piece now. Wouldn't another piece taste great. You've blown it, so why not mess it up good. Go ahead, have another piece and why not top it off with some vanilla ice cream?"

So you give in and feel terrible. Then comes Lie #3 which is the final stage of loss of control.

LIE #3
"GIVE UP"

By giving in and doing what you did not want to do you feel terrible. You have "messed it up good", so now the natural progression is to stop trying, simply "give up". What this lie tries to get you to say is "I'm worthless, I'm hopeless, I will never be able to control my habits. I'll quit trying."

Reject all three lies, they are false. Once is rarely enough. If you are tempted to do something wrong "once" check out if it's not the first of the three lies.

If you do mess something up, don't mess it up worse. You don't have to go any further. You can resume control. Exercise that control now. And never believe Lie #3, never quit trying. You are of immense value and you are never hopeless. The winners in life recognize and refute the lies of the Habit Demons. Jim Sharkey, a man who has had a tremendous impact on my life once said "No man is a loser until he quits trying."

2. IDENTIFYING PRESSURE

We all face a certain degree of pressure. It is a healthy thing in the right doses. This next list will help you identify pressure points in your life. Score yourself by order of present pressure.

X = The top pressure point for me (check only one X)
A = Causes pressure daily
B = Causes pressure sometimes
C = Causes pressure rarely

___Unrealistic expectations
___Failure to make tough decisions
___Procrastination
___Over commitment
___Job demands
___Change
___Work is unpleasant
___No guidance or support
___Pressure of competition
___Maintain current level of success
___Laziness
___Forgetfulness
___No drive
___Educational limitation
___Boredom
___Lack of knowledge
___Peer pressure
___Watch too much TV
___Interruptions
___People nagging
___Economy
___Negativity
___Back-logs of things to be done
___Traffic jams
___Travelling
___Waiting on others
___Perfectionism

___Getting started in the morning
___Workaholic tendencies
___Authors who ask too many questions
___Unresolved conflict
___Financial pressures
___Unexpected problems
___Recurring interpersonal friction
___Uncertain future
___Health problems
___In-laws
___Friends
___Worry
___Fear
___Religious involvement
___Other_____

Have you identified only one X? That is the number one thing you need to work on. Is it negative pressure? Is it within your ability to eliminate?

Come up with ten possible ways to relieve some of the pressure in the area you marked X. Think of ten possible solutions without evaluating them. This will get you thinking of solutions instead of problems. Now take make a plan to control the pressure. Once this is done start working on the A's.

10 POSSIBLE SOLUTIONS

1.   2.

3.   4.

5.   6.

7.   8.

9.   10.

3. IDENTIFYING THE MINUTE TAKER WASTERS

You have 86,400 seconds at your disposal everyday. You decide how you will use those seconds. What really impedes time effectiveness is the Minute Taker Wasters. The small things which creep into our day which eat up seconds which turn into minutes which turn into hours which turn into days ad infinitum. How do people waste time? If we can identify the Minute Taker Wasters we can develop a plan for effectiveness in removing the Operational success blockers.

MINUTE TAKER WASTERS

Shuffling paper

Self-interruptions

Coffee breaks

Looking for things

Sloppy desk

Terrible note taking

Forgetfulness

Piles of "stuff" on desk

Not have stock of regularly used items

Stock piling junk

Messy drawers

Borrowing things we should have on our desk

Telephone tag

Interruptions

Procrastinating

Getting going after interruptions

Meetings running on and on

Day dreaming

Re-scheduling appointments missed

Having to do something over because it was done wrong

Looking for things in the middle of a task

Too many "to do" lists

Transferring tasks from "to do" list to "to do" list

Television

Poor planning

Not scheduling enough time.

4. IDENTIFYING PRIORITIES QUICKLY

You have one hour to work on 15 things. You have no idea which is most important. You need a tool to help you prioritize which one you will work on first. You need a tool which will help you decide quickly the order of priorities for goals to set, items to work on, people to invite to a meeting, etc. The scale described below will help you identify in an instant an order of priorities.

This tool was developed by Colorado management consultant Myron Rush and has been used extensively to help thousands of managers to set priorities. It is without question, one of the most valuable priority setting tools available today. It is an effective instrument to assist in identifying which tasks are urgent and which ones are important. For some of us, we spend far too much time on the urgent items but they may not be the most important ones.

PRIORITY SCALE

Step 1. In the upper left hand corner, under "List", record and number the items you wish to prioritize.

Step 2. Compare item 1 with item 2 and circle the one which is most important. Next, compare 1 with 3, circling the most important. As you trade off between items what you want to determine is, "If I could only do 1 or 2 which one would I do?" You the circle the number you chose as most important between the two.

Continue the process by moving one row to the right and comparing item 2 with 3. Next compare 1 with 4 and 2 with 4, and so on.

Step 3. Once you have completed the comparison, add up the total number of 1's, 2's, 3's etc. and record the total.

Step 4. Now you are ready to rearrange the items in order of priority.

LIST   PRIORITIES

```
1                                    ___1's
2                                    ___2's
1  2                                 ___3's
3  3                                 ___4's
1  2  3                              ___5's
4  4  4                              ___6's
1  2  3  4                           ___7's
5  5  5  5                           ___8's
1  2  3  4  5                        ___9's
6  6  6  6  6
1  2  3  4  5  6
7  7  7  7  7  7
1  2  3  4  5  6  7
8  8  8  8  8  8  8
1  2  3  4  5  6  7  8
9  9  9  9  9  9  9  9
```

PRIORITY SCALE

1.   2.

3.   4.

5.   6.

7.   8.

9.

5. CONTROLLING PROCRASTINATION

> ## "PROCRASTINATION IS THE ONLY THING WE HAVE TIME FOR."

A doctor turned to his patient and said, "Bill, I have some bad news and some worse news." "Hold on now doctor", said the concerned patient, "I can handle bad news and good news but bad news and worse news?" The doctor asked which one he should share first. Bill wanted the bad news first. "Well", the doctor said sadly, "the results of all the tests are in and you only have 24 hours to live." "What? That's the bad news what could possibly be worse than that?" The doctor replied apologetically, "We found out yesterday and forgot to tell you."

It is relatively easy to come up with many excuses for putting things off. We don't have the time right now. I will get around to it later. Let me sleep on it first. There is lots of time to that this weekend. Why do we procrastinate?

The reason is quite simple! It is easy to put off the unpleasant, difficult and time-consuming tasks. In essence, procrastination is nothing more than a time waster. It causes many more headaches than it cures. Think right now of all the small tedious things you have procrastinated about in the past week, month, year, decade. They are all cramping your brain.

So we only do those tasks which scream the most, as it were. We rush to finish them. The minute we lick the envelope we notice we forgot to insert the letter. We start cooking hamburgers only to remember the B.B.Q. gas tank is empty. There is a cure for procrastination! Look in a mirror and you will see the cure. The only person who will manage you is You!

How To Handle Procrastination

1. START THE TASK.

Even if you have failed at it in the past. If you want to win, you must begin. This seems obvious but if you have been procrastinating at something, just make a start at it and you will have begun the process of success.

2. BLOCK OFF THE NECESSARY TIME TO FINISH THE JOB.

We will discuss this point in more detail in a later section in this chapter. Chances are very remote that you will ever get done without it getting scheduled into your calendar. We procrastinate for ever because we don't block off the necessary time to finish the job.

3. SEE THE JOB IN BITE SIZED PIECES.

You will never start losing weight if you see the whole project in one lump sum. An alcoholic could never picture himself not drinking for the rest of his/her life. They can handle not drinking for this 24 hour period. "One day at a time" is a popular slogan among self-help groups.

4. ADOPT A DO IT NOW MENTALITY.

People who conquer procrastination problems learn to become "Do It Now'ers". They never wait until tomorrow to do what they know should be done today. They put things back after each use. They refuse to delay.

5. SET OBJECTIVES.

We already discussed the need for objectives in life but it bears repeating here as it affects the procrastination dilemma. Set a goal to accomplish something you have procrastinated doing.

6. REVIEW ACCOMPLISHMENTS.

Winners in life dwell on their successes. Losers constantly focus in on their failures. It is of value to remind yourself of areas you have succeeded in winning the procrastination game.

7. REWARD OR PUNISH YOURSELF.

Now I am not espousing deviant behaviour by suggesting you conquer procrastination problems by punishing yourself. What I am suggesting is that you find some way of punishing negative behaviours like not doing things you said you would do.

One manager I know buys all his staff lunch, out of his own pocket, if he does not have his reports in on time. If he promises to deliver something and procrastinates, he has to fork out cash and for him this is negative reinforcement for negative behaviour.

Similarly if you have succeeded in doing a task you have long procrastinated in doing, reward yourself. We tend to repeat those behaviours with positive reinforcements and shun the negatives reinforcers.

Procrastination Worksheet

Things I put off doing:

How does this make me feel?

Is it important?

      Yes (Why?)

      No (Why not?)

Action plan

1.

2.

3.

4.

6. RE-THINKING INTERRUPTIONS

5 STEPS TO HANDLING INTERRUPTIONS

If interruptions are a problem for you, consider using the 5 steps listed below. The way to determine what is a problem with interruptions ask yourself, "Am I receiving low-priority interruptions during high-priority projects?" If so, consider practising these steps to curb the time wasting interruptions.

STEP 1
SCHEDULE CLOSED DOOR PERIODS.

Many people think the only time you are really "busy" is when you have a person with you. A secretary looks into an executive's office sees no one and falsely assumes that he is available.

There is nothing wrong with scheduling time in your daily planner which will allow you avoid the time wasting activity called interruptions.

STEP 2
LET OTHERS KNOW YOU CANNOT BE INTERRUPTED.

If you want to eliminate interruptions, schedule closed door "uninterruption" periods. Let others know you can't be bothered for any other reason than the building is on fire. And only if the fire is approaching the floor below, at that.

STEP 3
IF INTERRUPTED STAND UP.

Do you want a technique that is guaranteed to cut interruption time in half? Stand up as soon as an interrupter enters the room. Simply stand up while they speak. They will soon get the message, "Be quick, I'm busy".

If someone enters a room to interrupt you and you invite them in and sit comfortably, put your feet up on the desk, offer them a coffee, what message do you think you are conveying to them? "Sure come on in, let's talk, what I was doing isn't really important. Use my time in any way you see fit."

STEP 4.
AVOID EYE CONTACT.

Ergonomic experts are now realizing the importance of eye contact in office design. It plays a role in employee productivity. They are now designing offices to ensure less eye contact.

I have been on the telephone speaking to someone long distance, someone walks by my office and because we make eye contact they feel free to start speaking to me at the same time. It blows my mind.

So one way to lower interruptions is to make less eye contact with people. This is particularly true with telephones. Be sure to face a wall while on the telephone.

STEP 5.
MAKE FEWER TRIPS THROUGH THE OFFICE.

Now this may seem a bit trivial but are you aware how much time is wasted in a day by running for a coffee, water and the washroom? What I am suggesting is becoming aware that when you leave your work area you are a prime target to get sidetracked.

7. GETTING THE MOST FROM YOUR DAILY PLANNER

Here is a random list of the most common mistakes people make when it comes to their personal daily planners or daily calendar.

- Having more than one.
- Not carrying it with them at all times.
- Not writing everything down in it.
- Not writing the telephone number of the person they have appointments with in case of cancellations.
- Not having post-it notes, 3 x 5 cards, paper clips, and other office supplies with their planner.
- Failing to schedule personal as well as business related events.
- Not allocating enough time to finish the job.
- Not blocking off task times to finish projects.
- Depending on "to do" lists instead of actually blocking off the time.
- Not re-scheduling events that are postponed or cancelled.

8. FREEING YOUR MIND (B.F. SYSTEM)

So much time is wasted wading through piles of paper and remembering letters and reports. The B.F. (Bring Forward) System I am recommending is nothing revolutionary, but very few people use it. Many time management experts recommend using this type of system to free your mind, relying on a retrieval system instead of your memory.

The system has two sets of files, one for each month and one for the 31 days of the month. To set up this B.F. system, you will need twelve manilla file folders; one for every month of the year.

You will also need 31 folders marked, in large print, 1 to 31, representing every day of the month. Here is how the system works. Let's say I have to speak at a convention on the 12th of next month. I always fill out a "booking worksheet" for every speaking engagement. It outlines such vital information as what time on, what time off. It covers audience analysis, meeting planner objectives, location of talk, room-set up etc.. I take that sheet, stick it into the file marked 12, and do not worry about it again until the 12th of next month. I simply check the system everyday.

If a prospect asks me to call back next July, I drop a card with the customer's request into the July file and don't worry about it until then. At the start of each month, I empty the monthly file into the respective daily file and relax. The monthly files are rotated monthly but the daily files stay in the same order. I can retrieve information in an instant.

9. TACKLING THE TELEPHONE

Having a keen interest in sales and sales training, I have discovered that this nice little box we call the telephone can be a real time saver or it can be a real time waster. Let me share the findings of our research as to the top 10 mistakes made over the telephone.

1. Give control to whom you are speaking.
2. Speak too long.
3. Speak to the wrong person.
4. Poor or no note taking.
5. Not grouping calls together
6. Shuffling paper during calls.
7. Waste time between calls.
8. Poor planning before calling.
9. Not asking when the best time to call back.
10. Not calling.

10. IMPLEMENTING TIME SAVERS

Implement at least 20 of these 60 practical time savers by placing a check mark beside the ones you will start first.

**60
PRACTICAL
TIME MANAGEMENT TIPS**

---

1. When cleaning out closets, storerooms etc, label three cartons "scrap", "give away", and "keep".

2. If you haven't used something for over a year, don't let it take up prime space.

3. Schedule a "quiet hour" each day and consider it non-negotiable.

4. Don't let others infringe on your valuable "prime-time".

5. Each evening get out everything you will need in the morning.

6. Use your planning calendar to schedule your "to do" lists.

7. Schedule "appointments" with yourself.

8. Have an office in your home for writing and filing.

9. Take advantage of self-inking stamps to conserve time.

10. Delegate whenever possible.

11. Get things done during commuting time.

12. Make up casseroles in double quantity and freeze them.

13. Throw out as much correspondence and other paperwork as possible.

14. Store jewellery in egg cartons inside a drawer.

15. Maintain a stock of frequently used items such as papergoods, light-bulbs, garbage bags, paper clips, post it's.

16. Make minor decisions quickly.

17. Don't waste time agonizing after decisions.

18. Store items close to where they will be used. Duplicate where necessary.

19. Clean the bathtub during a shower. It is easier working from the inside.

20. Keep desk supplies in your briefcase or car for those unpredictable delays and waiting periods.

21. Say "no" more often. Stop volunteering for everything.

22. Don't keep shuffling paper. Handle each one as it appears.

23. Start earlier in the morning.

24. Don't read passively. Search for ideas. Use highlighters. Make marginal notes.

25. Don't store magazines. Tear out or photocopy relevant articles.

26. Set a deadline on all tasks and stick to it.

27. Always carry a small scratch pad with you for notetaking.

28. Plan in advance your TV viewing time. It can be a real time robber.

29. Use coloured labels to flag important dates in your planning calendar to highlight urgent requests that come up.

30. Carry a supply of "post-its" notes in your planning calendar.

31. Review "junk mail" during low energy times (ie the last 15 minutes of the day).

32. Take only carry on bags while travelling in airports. Delays occur when waiting for checked bags.

33. Use only transparent containers for left-overs so you can see what you have in the refrigerator.

34. When leaving a message to call you back, indicate the best time to call you back.

35. If the person you call is not there, try to get the information you need from someone else rather than leave a message to call back.

36. Keep paper and pen handy in every room.

37. Carry a portable "Trident" 3-hole punch (1 1/2" wide x 10 1/4" long x 3/8" thick) in your briefcase or meeting binder.

38. Record the time you must leave the house in your planning calendar when you must attend meetings some distance away.

39. Have more keys made than you think you'll need.

40. Don't be a slave to your telephone. Take messages during the dinner hour -- or ignore it completely.

41. Make doctor and dentist appointments first thing in the morning so you're ahead of the crowd.

42. Keep a supply of greeting cards and stamps on hand. Also gifts.

43. Put away materials immediately after use. Clean up the mess as it's generated.

44. Use a highlighter when reading letters, reports, etc., so you can mark those parts requiring action.

45. Always confirm appointments; don't assume the other person will remember.

46. Use stacking trays to sort mail as to bills, correspondence, junk mail.

47. Place coloured dots on all your credit cards for easy identification.

48. Photocopy both sides of your credit cards (about nine per page) and leave a copy at your home and office as well as carry one with you.

49. Use driving time to listen to cassette tapes.

50. Record ideas from cassette tapes by dictating into a pocket recorder.

51. Keep a pocket recorder in your car for recording ideas, information, things to do, etc., as they occur to you.

52. Subscribe to newsletters related to your profession to cut down on reading time.

53. Colour code your various keys with small plastic rings available in many stores to avoid fumbling for the right key.

54. Photocopy birth certificates, marriage certificates, etc., and keep them in your files.

55. Form the habit of taking your planning calendar with you wherever you go -- even on vacation. You can record those ports of call, favourite restaurants, hotels, people you meet, etc.

56. Store empty clothes hangers to one side of the closet and use as required. Don't let them mix with used ones.

57. Keep a personal effects tote bag equipped with all personal items from toothbrush to travel hair dryer and use it only for travelling.
58. Find ways to delegate more.
59. Shorten telephone calls.
60. Phone instead of writing.

USE YOUR TIME WISELY

> "When a young man sits on a hot stove, a minute seems like an hour. But when a beautiful girl sits on that young man's lap, an hour seems like a minute."
>
> **Albert Einstein**

CHAPTER 8

RELAX MAN, RELAX!
How To Handle Stress and Avoid Burn-out

S tress can cause us to do the most stupid things imaginable. A bricklayer was under considerable stress because he was running late for a special date with a new girlfriend. He did not want to keep her waiting on this his second date.

He was repairing the top of a brick building. He rigged a hoist and a boom, attached a rope to a barrel and pulled bricks to the top. When they reached the roof, he secured the rope at the bottom. Because he was rushed for time, he made some wrong decisions. He decided that he would speed up the clean up time by loading all the spare bricks on the roof top into the wheel barrel. He went down and released the rope to lower the bricks. What he did not realize was that the barrel, full of bricks, now weighed considerably more than he did. So, he grabbed the rope and up he went. Halfway up, he met the barrel coming down and broke his nose and one shoulder.

Still he hung on and went all the way to the top, hitting his head on the boom and jamming his fingers in the pulley. By this time the barrel full of bricks hit the bottom, spilling all the bricks, making the barrel considerably lighter than he was. So down he came and up the barrel went. Halfway down, he met the barrel coming up and cracked both ankles. But still he hung on to the rope attached to the empty barrel which was now at the top of the building. And to prove that an idiot under stress has no limit to his idiocy, he let go of the rope, releasing the empty barrel which crowned him on the head.

THE NATURE OF STRESS IN LAYMAN'S TERMS

MY SEVEN STRESS FRIENDS

MR. CANT SLOWDOWN

I would like to introduce you to my friend Cant but he's hard to nail down, even for an introduction. He's a mover and a shaker. He's busy, motivated and busy. Did I mention busy? Yeah he is busy.

This guy is so busy he'll put stuff in his calendar just to avoid the guilt he feels when he has nothing to do. Well, really he never has nothing to do because he's so busy. The only time he is free from the telephone is the walk from the front porch to the car. The only time he isn't meeting someone is the time he "wastes" taking a shower. Although he's seriously considering putting a phone in there too. He is president of the Lion's Club, chairman of the elders board at church, volunteer for the Cancer Society, sits on 218 committees at work, heads the fire brigade for the office tower and holds three dozen more positions or offices of importance.

MRS. I. M. AMARTYR

You may have already met her. She no doubt has greeted you at the PTA meeting, or was it at the garage sale raising money for the refugees? She has a bleeding heart for every cause under the sun. If you are having a problem, with anything, Mrs. Amartyr is the one to call. If you need anything from milk to counselling she is available. I know she is available because whenever I call she's busy giving something to someone somewhere. She just gives and gives and gives. She always puts others first.

Now that's sort of funny. She seems to care about everyone else's welfare except her own. Hey, now that I think about it, she's at least 50 lbs. overweight. She's always giving but who's caring about her? I wonder.

MRS. DIS CONTENT

You will love her. She has lots and lots of beautiful stuff. You should see her house. They have so many cars, I lost count. Her furs and diamonds really identify her as a high achiever. She has a special case for all her credit cards. She uses them all too.

She has 2 subscriptions to every catalogue in the world. I wonder if that runs in her family? This lady works hard. Now you can learn a lot from Mrs. Dis Content. For example, if you studied her behaviour you could learn how to use people and love things. You could learn how to be so dissatisfied with life that you are willing to risk all the important things just to satisfy the empty feelings on the inside. She's a lovely lady from far but far from lovely.

MR. HATE QUIET

Wherever he goes, noise accompanies him. It's funny how that happens. Someone said he has a hard time with silence. I disagreed. It's just that he loves music, loud music. He loves the "white noise". I'm a lot like Mr. Hate Quiet. Oh, by the way, it's not true that he watches the football game on television, listens to the baseball game on the radio and listens to a Walkman cassette player all at the same time. No way, he hates football, it's tennis!

MR. NOTME

Mr. Notme is one of my best friends. He has no problems. No really! He is never rushed, never gets upset. He hasn't bought into the "Stress Trip" like you and me. He's always calm and cool. He is a rock. This guy is smooth.

When you meet him you'll notice his hair is somewhat unusual. It is perfect. This guy has never had a hair out of place in the past 37 years. He is never bothered by the stress and hurriedness that you and I suffer from. He is the guy everyone wants on their committees. He makes up for all the jerks. He has nothing but nice things to say about everyone at all times.

Something does puzzle me about him though, I saw Mr. Notme leave the clinic for people with chronic ulcers. I wonder if he had anything to do with Mrs. Notme's black eye? Nah, not Mr. Notme.

MRS. LOOK ATME

No one can touch her in the achievement department. Somebody told me what a difficult childhood she had, but has really accomplished a lot since then. She is one of the most open people I have ever met. In fact, when I went to her house for the first time, (second and third time too, for that matter), she showed me everything she owned. How kind of her!

She wasn't bragging though. No, she's just happy with all she's been able to do more than everyone else. I laughed when she said to me, "I've been talking about myself for an hour now, how about you talk about me some." She's funny that way!

You might know my friends already. They may be influencing your life in fact. If so we have something in common. Great! Let's see if we can put them in proper focus in this chapter on dealing with stress and burnout.

Many great and extraordinary discoveries and advances are being made in medicine and the health sciences relating to stress. This chapter is not written from a medical point of view. I am not a doctor. I am a classic Type A personality, who is interested in understanding and controlling the negative aspects of stress to prevent burn-out which will allow me to achieve my full potential and enjoy life. It is from this perspective that I address this subject.

The word "stress" conjures up different things in the minds of different people. It is a multifaceted response that includes changes in perception, emotion, behaviour and physical functioning. There are positive and negative sides to stress. We could say that only dead people have no stress. We need a certain amount of it to function.

I am not qualified to speak about all the physical effects that stress can have on our bodies. It is common knowledge, however, that distress affects our bodies. It contributes to illness, emotional disorders, sleep problems, performance issues and the list can go on and on. Not all stress is bad! Some of us thrive on it. It gives some people a sense of exhilaration. It can fire us up and it can bring out the best in us.

SYMPTOMS OF DISTRESS

Let me share some commonly accepted symptoms of distress.

- Wake up feeling tired.
- Experience many colds.
- Heartbeat seems to race or is irregular.
- Have many headaches.
- Nervousness shown in trembling hands or nervous tics.
- Skin diseases.

- Intestinal disorders such as indigestion, diarrhoea, and constipation.
- Insomnia.
- Excessive perspiration.
- Irritable or angry often.
- General feeling of pain. (Back pain, stomach, muscles, head pains, etc.)
- Restlessness, can't sit still for very long.
- Increase in anxiety.
- Feet and hands are cold.
- Increase in allergies.
- Sexual difficulties.
- Family conflict.
- Feel pressured at work, home, church, community groups.
- Short tempered.
- Relationship problems.
- Isolation.
- Compulsive behaviours.
- Memory loss.
- Easily irritated or annoyed.
- Excessive mental fantasy life.
- Very critical of others.

TEST YOUR STRESS LEVELS

Think about the past year. What we want you to rate in this test is the amount of change that has occurred in the past 12 months. Use the following scale by choosing the number which reflects your current feelings.

0 = Not true whatsoever in my case
5 = Slightly true of me
6 = Generally true of me
7 = Extremely true of me

_____ 1. I sometimes wake up tired and exhausted.
_____ 2. I worry about people, work, things somewhat.
_____ 3. I avoid people on occasion.
_____ 4. I am cynical at times.
_____ 5. I am critical of myself.
_____ 6. I have more headaches than before.
_____ 7. My sense of humour is not what it used to be.
_____ 8. I have gastrointestinal problems.
_____ 9. I sometimes feel tired and worn-out.
_____ 10. I am somewhat critical of others.
_____ 11. I am less spontaneous.
_____ 12. My sex drive has changed somewhat.
_____ 13. I sometimes have less control of habits.
_____ 14. I feel like I'm at the end of my rope at times.
_____ 15. I have somewhat less ambition.
_____ 16. I seem to forget things more.
_____ 17. I sometimes desire time alone.
_____ 18. I'm sick more often.
_____ 19. I don't treat people as well as I should at times.
_____ 20. I am somewhat pessimistic.

_____ **TOTAL SCORE**

WHAT IT ALL MEANS!

1 to 20	Are you alive? You may be taking things a little too casually.
21 to 50	The normal zone.
51 to 70	The caution sign. The early signs of distress and burnout are showing. Consider relaxing some.
71 to 80	The hot district. It may be time for you to take some action to get things under control before too long.
81 to 89	The burn-out area. You are about to skid all over the map. You must reevaluate your life and get serious help now.
90 +	Danger Zone. You are threatening the condition of your well being. Unless you change the course of your life you will experience serious dangers in the very near future.

HOW TO PREVENT BURN-OUT
4 POWERFUL WORDS

ACKNOWLEDGE

The first step in any program of self-improvement is usually the acknowledgement phase. To get better at something the first thing you have to realize is that you may just have a problem. If you scored over 70 on the above Stress Test, you should consider acknowledging a potential problem in your life.

We don't like to admit we have a problem or difficulty in our life. By not recognizing and acknowledging the pressure and stress we face and the way we deal with it, we may steer our ships right into the reef of disaster. The reef of relationship disaster or the reef of physical disaster or vocational or financial disaster.

THINKING

To avoid the burn-out trap you should consider the thinking that accompanies it. People about to crash think without stopping. Their minds are like horses out in the field; running and running and jumping and jumping. They are constantly solving, considering, thinking, pondering, planning, scheming and working inside their minds.

They are also thinking rapidly. They maintain a pace that would kill the average person. They leave others in the dust. They often reach the finish line before others even leave the blocks. They think about and work on several projects at the same time. They think in multi-dimensional ways. They have an amazing ability to think on different levels at the same time.

People who fit this description move from one mental project to another with ease. They can simultaneously think about a new project and consider what to say at tomorrow's Rotary meeting. The difference between these people and brilliant thinkers is the issue of control. Who's in control of the thought process? Can they slowdown voluntarily or can they exercise little or no control?

Without slowing down that thinking and having brain drains throughout the day you will continue to suffer the effects of expending so much energy. Some experts suggest mentally slowing down the pace of thought. Practice (if you can find the time!) thinking about only one thing at a time.

ATTITUDE

This "hurry-hurry" syndrome may have a lot to do with our attitudes. What is our attitude about our place in life. Are we trying to prove something to ourselves or others? What causes certain people to behave in ways that science has proven to be harmful, even fatal? What's our attitude toward the speed at which things should get done? What causes us to live with a fanatical sense of urgency? Perhaps that's what this whole book is about - awareness of attitudes.

When it comes to avoiding burn-out, the buzz word is slow down. (I just typed that sentence in less than 4 seconds and it's 1 a.m.. I must meet a deadline for tomorrow at 7:30 a.m..)

HABITS

This point was covered in a previous chapter. People who live long lives have certain behaviours which allows them to live healthy, happy lives. They have control of their personal habits. They have developed healthy habits and positive behaviours like...

- Laughing a lot.
- Resting a lot.
- Relaxing some.
- Eating right.
- Playing hard.
- Slowing their pace down some.
- Develop pingthe spiritual disciplines.
- Expressing emotion well.
- Venting anger.
- Being aware of the danger zones.

"THEY CAN
BECAUSE
THEY THINK THEY CAN."
Virgil

CONQUERING
THE
RELATIONAL
SUCCESS-BLOCKERS

CHAPTER 9

STEPS
TO
SUPERIOR HUMAN
RELATIONS!

The ability to relate well with others is one of the most important skills a person can have to enjoy success in life. To be a good performer or a good salesman, a good parent or a good friend, a good manager or a good politician, what you really need is the ability to form powerful common human bonds and relationships of responsiveness.

Why are some people so desirable to be around? There are people who we naturally gravitate to. Why? Why do certain people attract us, while others cause seemingly endless irritation for us?

The secret of enjoying success is to remove the barriers to strong and powerful human relations. Give a little, you get a little back. Give a lot, you get a lot back. This is the law of proportionate return. Whatever you give away will always come back to you!

THE RELATIONSHIP TREE

The "Relationship Tree" is the model for this next chapter. It serves as a metaphor to describe the elements of healthy relationships. Relationships are like trees. When one of the elements suffer the whole tree suffers. The growth of a tree is very similar to what happens in strong, developing relationships.

The Soil - Environment

The soil determines whether a tree shrivels or stretches. It covers the roots, that feed the tree. The soil is either an environment that brings forth nourishment or death and disease. It causes the tree to flourish or whither away; strengthens or starves.

Similarly, the environment of relationships determine whether they bring health and happiness or whether it prevents the needed nutrition from producing growth. To be fertile, soil must have certain characteristics which are conducive to giving life and health. For a relationship to thrive it must be surrounded by words that uplift rather than create emotional, mental, and spiritual death. Words have the power to contaminate a self-image.

WORDS

"SUCCESS DOESN'T ALWAYS GO TO THE HEAD.
SOMETIMES IT GOES TO THE MOUTH."

Arnold H. Glasow

The task of leaders is to communicate words that will produce growth. It probably wouldn't hurt to reiterate my strong feeling that the best place to start communicating is to ourselves. We need to surround ourselves with words that strengthen and feed us. The next step is to examine the words we use with others. I look at my son Corey, smile and say, "No" politely or I can just as easily devastate him by screaming making a mean and distorted grimace, "Noooooo!!!".

The prime performers in relationships are very aware how they speak to others. For example, by changing the emphasis, I create four different meanings from the same sentence.

- <u>DID</u> he steal the money?
- Did <u>HE</u> steal the money?
- Did he <u>STEAL</u> the money?
- Did he steal the <u>MONEY</u>?

Mark Twain said he could live two months on a good compliment. A good friend, who happens to be a very good and hard worker complained to me recently that she had worked very hard for her company without even one word of recognition. Take a guess, do you think she is still working there? Nope! What a loss. That company missed out on one of the best people they ever had.

Perhaps this is the place to briefly touch on the subject of put down humour which is nothing more than laughter at the expense of others. Well, that's brief enough.

CREATIVITY

When soil is full of vibrant life it is very creative. The same can be said of solid, healthy, growing relationships. Practice what I call creative silliness.

The next time you drive through a toll gate, pay for the person behind you. It'll blow their mind. Call up a pizza shop and ask them if they would like anything. Call 411, directory assistance and give her a number. Put a sandwich in your mailbox for the postman. Put 300 post-it notes on the wall saying why you value the relationship or simply "I LUV U".

Up to this point you thought that I was on the ball but I surely lost my faculties here, right? Well, not to worry. Life is so short. We are so stuffy about having fun. Let's celebrate a little!

RECOGNITION

Acknowledgement is to relationships what hydrogen is to soil. It brings life and joy to relationships. Think of some accomplishment when you were recognized and rewarded. Wow! You felt great. We all need to be praised, even the most confident of us.

I was writing Dr. Schuller and thought I should give him a compliment and acknowledge his stellar conduct and fortitude during the television scandals which no doubt affected his ministry.

I was really proud that he didn't pack it in or become bitter. I wanted to tell him but hesitated because I thought, "This guy probably gets thousands of letters every week telling him how great he is, he doesn't need me to tell him?" Then I wondered what if he didn't, then again what if he did, so what? He deserves recognition, so he got it.

Practical Guidelines For Effective Recognition.

- Praise people specifically.
- Praise people repeatedly.
- Praise people honestly.
- Praise people publicly.

Why not send a thank you card today? Acknowledge a graduation? Remember a birthday or anniversary? Publicly recognize the hard work of others. Say, "You Matter" to someone today?

You can make more friends in two months by becoming interested in them than you can in two years trying to get them interested in you.

ENVIRONMENT

Soil is environment. What kind of environment are you creating for your relationships? What atmosphere are you generating? Yes, you generate an atmosphere even if your not the boss. Do people like being around you?

Maybe it's time to realize you are responsible for the environment your relationships find themselves. Are they in good soil? Is it possible for the life giving nutrients to feed the whole tree? What can you do, regardless of the present environment, to make being around you better?

The Roots - Acceptance

Roots go out into the soil and collect the vital ingredients for growth and deliver them to the rest of the tree. Without healthy roots a tree cannot stand firm in the storms. There is no way it can absorb the nourishment necessary to produce life in the tree.

Acceptance is the vehicle by which health producing nutrition is delivered. Without acceptance in relationships we doubt and like roots in a drought forage deeper and deeper until our need is met. For some people this endless search for acceptance leads to terrible patterns in relationships. A victim of domestic abuse leaves one abuser only to hook up with another. He provides acceptance and that's what she needs, wants and gets; regardless of the cost. A child who lives without acceptance behaves in ways that is obvious to everyone but to the person who should be acknowledging them and giving them acceptance.

Many experts in the field of psychology and counselling have discovered that we have immense needs for security and significance. We want to know we are of worth, and there is a sense of security in our lives. Relationships that meet these needs allow other health and happiness producing ingredients to flow about the tree. If the root is damaged, diseased or not existing the tree will die. The same is true with relationships.

I often share what I looked like in 1977, the day I made a decision to turn my life around. I had long hair, leather jackets, big motorcycle, scruffy jeans. I had an exterior which said, "stay away I am an ugly, mean person," but on the inside, I was just a kid in need of some acceptance. I had very little "acceptance" root. People like Norman Sharkey, Bob Marwick and Al Cameron fixed the root by accepting me just the way I was.

They made no demands, they saw beyond the harsh exterior to the hurting and needy interior. If it wasn't for these men I'm not sure where I'd be today. I owe my life to these champions of acceptance.

The Trunk - Strength For The Storms

What is the strongest part of the tree? The trunk. What is the best defence against the fierce storms of life? A strong, unshakable trunk. Everything else can fall away but it's the trunk that will stand on for ever. What hope do branches and leaves have without a powerful trunk?

A lady in one of my seminars said that when she found out she had leukemia, a deadly form of cancer, everyone avoided her. Her whole support team in life, packed up shop and hit the road. How tragic. The time she needed her friends the most they could not be found. They found her pain and illness too difficult. It's during these storms of life, which hit us all, that trunks, solid trunks are developed in relationships.

In 1986, I heard Tom Jones say on T.V. that "Elvis Presley would still be alive if he had more close friends." My greatest friends today are the ones who built during the storms of my life. I got a call from Edmonton that my twenty-seven year old brother had died. The darkest day of my life; July 21, 1978. It was the people who during that hurricane stayed with me and supported me who I count as the most valuable, solid friends I have today.

During the trials and tough times of life don't shun people, go to them. You will build strong bonds that will last a lifetime. And like trunks, your relationships will be able to withstand the next storm even stronger.

A true story is told a man who answered a newspaper column asking when a father should stop hugging his teenage boys. The article said that a dad should never stop. He shared that just the day before he hugged and kissed his teenage boy for the first time. But it was too late. The boy had just committed suicide. The father felt that during the storms of the teenager's life he neglected to be there and do whatever he could to strengthen their relationship. He had apparently grown up believing that affection, love, communication was the commodity of cowards. He discovered, too late, the opposite to be true.

The Branches - Performance

It would be true to say branches are the most visible parts of the tree. They are what people see the most of. They hold the leaves. Collectively they are the biggest part of most trees but individually they are the smallest. Now here is an interesting parallel. Performance, our behaviour and that of others is what we see first. It is the biggest part of what people observe and remember. Behaviour makes up a large part of relationships. What we need to keep in perspective is that individually, performance is only a part of a whole.

We need to get perspective on performance. If my behaviour will threaten our relationship, the relationship will be on shaky ground. I consult with many Fortune 500 companies on how to improve and manage the performance of employees so let me be perfectly clear when I address the subject of performance.

I am not suggesting even for a moment that inappropriate behaviour be overlooked or even tolerated. What I am suggesting is that in relationships if I have to "earn" your friendship by what I do or don't do the relationship will be shallow. The security of the relationship should not rest on behaviour. I advocate the security of the relationship rest on commitment.

This also includes wrongful comparisons people make to judge whether or not they accept, love or relate with others. As we compare what others should and shouldn't do to be accepted, we often do so against the image of "successful" people. These images are often unrealistic or idealistic. Unfortunately we measure other people's performance by them. They are often unattainable standards that prevent the beauty of branches and leaves to be seen.

For sure, people need to be encouraged to behave properly. But when it comes to acceptance, choose to base the relationship on commitment not behaviour.

The Bark - Rapport

The outer layer of a tree is called the bark. It protects against the elements. It is what people see on the exterior. A heathy bark requires that all the other elements of the tree are functioning properly. The bark, however, can just as easily kill the tree if it is not healthy.

Rapport is the ability to be in sync with another person. That is, to relate in a way that is characterized by common bonds. You feel united and "together"; that's rapport. Nothing is more frustrating when communicating with someone than feeling they are not responding. At times they seem uncomfortable and communication is difficult. It is possible to develop the skills necessary to turn that around. These techniques will be covered now and in more detail in the following chapter, when we discuss the topic of conflict resolution.

MATCH AND MIRROR

Matching or mirroring has been around for years in different philosophical circles and movements. Neuro-Linguistic Programming (NLP) suggests this technique to create commonality which enhances our ability to install rapport, thereby relating and communicating more effectively with others.

What the principle suggests is that people relate best with people who are like they are. For example, if you want to establish rapport with someone you could mirror, that is reflect back to them, an interest they have, or someone they know, some idiosyncrasies or some behaviour which they do.

On more than one occasion, unfortunately, I have isolated people and hampered my communicative ability because I did not match or mirror the behaviour of people I was trying to sell to.

I am a fairly loud, bubbly, enthusiastic type of guy. I can recall once trying to sell a vice-president of a national real estate company my services as a sales trainer. I was shown into the man's office. He came in, walking very slowly. His deep voice was he checked his watch seven times in twenty minutes. I was delighted to have such a high level interview; he was second in command. Without thinking, I began my sales presentation at my normal fast pace. The pitch of my voice was high, my enthusiasm was five miles above his. Needless to say I could sense we were not connecting. I changed strategy. When I did, I saw him become much more interested and the interview last well over an hour with positive results.

When I realized we were not "in-tune". I stopped, paused, then posed a question. My voice was lower and the pace was exactly like his. "Mr. Vice-President, if you were me, what questions would you be asking right now?" Also, I matched his physiology. Without being obvious I matched with my body what he was doing with his. I couldn't believe the change in the man.

One of the best books I have ever read on this subject, and I highly recommend to everyone who is serious about success in life is the national best-seller, Unlimited Power by Anthony Robbins. This man's philosophy, books and live seminar changed my life. He sure doesn't need my endorsement but anyone with such leading edge and positive technologies has my support.

FLEXIBILITY

Pat Sajak is a different interviewer than Sam Donaldson. Dick Cavett interviews differently than Merv Grifith. If you wanted to sell something to these four people you would have to change your approach for each. The same is true in every situation where you want to attract success. The key is flexibility.

Everyone of us fall into one of four categories of social or personality styles. Each style has differences in pace, dress, desires, fears and particular annoyances. The key to establishing rapport is to relate to others based on their preferences not ours. Let's look at the factors which indicate what style people fit into. There are two primary factors: Influence and Emotion.

INFLUENCE AND EMOTION

Influence deals with assertiveness or how much energy a person will use to influence a situation. A person with a low influence rating does more asking then telling. A person with a high rating wants to direct and be in-charge.

The emotion rating indicates just how much a person shares of their feelings or emotion. Are they withholding, do you have to pull information out of them or do they let you know what's going on inside of them? Depending where you rate yourself on both of those factors will indicate which personality style you are.

THE THINKER

Dick Cavett is a Thinker. So is Spock from Star Trek and William F. Buckley. These people are analytical. When buying a car Thinkers ask about fuel economy first. Analytical share very little emotion and prefer to ask questions than make statements. They want to be correct. They also fear embarrassment. Thinkers are concerned with the bottom-line and are annoyed by surprises.

If ever stuck in a trapped elevator, The Thinkers stay calm, say little, quickly begin calculating how long they are delayed and record every single detail of the ordeal. They prefer to simply wait for help to come. They wish the Socializers would stop being so bossy and put those roof tiles back.

THE COMMANDER

Sam Donaldson is a Commander. So is Barbara Walters and Lou Grant from the Mary Tyler Moore Show. They are also called Drivers. They buy big black authoritative cars. Commanders like to be in-charge. Extreme commanders share very little of their own feelings. They are the people who prefer telling to asking. They are fast paced, concerned with results, fear loss of control and are annoyed by indecision.

Needless to say commanders would love the challenge of getting stuck in an elevator. They would not express fear but quickly start planning their escape. They would decide who would do what. Generally they would let the Socializer try his all his "half-baked" solutions before taking control of the situation.

Once "in-charge" they would probably not lose it. They would orchestrate the solutions.

THE SUPPORTER

Merv Grifith is a Supporter. So is Jimmy Carter and Marcus Welby. They are also called Amiables or Relaters. What kind of cars do you think these people buy? Station wagons and mini-vans so they can take more people. Supporters share much emotion and feeling in order to be liked and influence very little, preferring to let you have your way and creating less waves in the relationship. They are people orientated. They want to relate. They are pleasant, they want to be liked, they dislike any confrontation, and are annoyed by impatience.

In a trapped elevator, Socializer's would try and smooth the situation. They would probably try making jokes. They would attempt to bridge any hard feelings. The last thing they want is for the Thinkers to start fighting with the Commanders. They would be working hard to reconcile everyone. If anyone would suggest a sing song, it would be the Supporter.

THE SOCIALIZER

Pat Sajak is a SOCIALIZER. Other Socializers include Dr. Ruth, Johnny Carson, and Burt Reynolds. Guess who buys the red-hot, flashy sports car? Socializers or Expressives as they are commonly called share a great deal of emotion but unlike the Supporter they are fairly assertive. They want to be admired, fear loss of prestige and are annoyed by boredom.

Who do you think jumps for the telephone on a trapped elevator? He starts shouting and ordering the building management to get them out of there or else face a ten million dollar lawsuit? The Socializer wants to be seen as a "big-shot", so he dreams up about 340 possible solutions to get everyone off this elevator. They express either wholehearted support for alternative solutions to get people out or they vocalize a strong, loud, obstinate, hard-headed, obnoxious, feverish, opinionated opposition.

Want to attract success? Adapt your behaviour to match those of the people you want to influence. I am a feelings type of person. I wouldn't get very far with a Thinker unless I geared my communication with them to their likes, dislikes, fear and annoying issues.

THE STYLES TEST - WHAT ARE YOU?

Check each one that applies to you.

Column No. 1

_____Fears loss of control
_____Aloof
_____Reserved
_____Likes to be in-charge
_____Detailed in work
_____Annoyed by indecision
_____Careful in sharing opinions
_____Organized
_____Cautious
_____Formal in dress and speech
_____Decides quickly
_____Tells as opposed to asks
_____Seems difficult to get to know
_____Controlled body language
_____Very businesslike

_____TOTAL CHECKED FOR COLUMN NO. 1

Column No. 2

_____Aggressive
_____Assertive
_____Strong Opinions
_____Take charge attitude
_____Somewhat of a "name-dropper"
_____Tells as opposed to asks
_____Speaks in "feelings"
_____Talkative
_____Hates routine or boredom
_____Prefers faster pace
_____Mingles socially with ease
_____Outgoing
_____Firm handshake
_____Impulsive
_____Dramatic or flashy

_____TOTAL CHECKED FOR COLUMN NO. 2

Column No. 3

_____Hates arguing or confrontation
_____Friendships are extremely important
_____Patient
_____Reveals true self
_____Friendly
_____Decides with heart as opposed to head
_____Warm
_____Approachable
_____Annoyed by impatience
_____Uses opinions
_____Informal dress and speech
_____Likes relating to people
_____Very supportive
_____Seems easy to get to know
_____Easy going with self and others

_____TOTAL CHECKED FOR COLUMN NO. 3

Column No. 4

_____Prefers facts to feelings
_____Soft spoken
_____Not very critical of others
_____Pace slow
_____Doesn't feel comfortable taking chances
_____Indifferent handshake
_____Annoyed by surprises
_____Asks questions
_____Lets others take social initiative
_____Tends to avoid use of power
_____Go along attitude
_____Cooperative
_____Deliberate actions
_____Quiet
_____Moderate opinions

_____**TOTAL CHECKED FOR COLUMN NO. 4**

FIGURING OUT YOUR PERSONALITY STYLE

Add the total for each column. Subtract column 1 from the total
of column 3. Then subtract the total from column 2 from the total
of column 4. You then will have two figures. Place the first one
on the vertical line in the box and the second figure on the
appropriate place on the horizontal line.

TOTAL COLUMN 1: _____
TOTAL COLUMN 3: _____ (subtract from No. 1)
                    _____
(mark vertical line beside this number on the next page)

TOTAL COLUMN 2: _____
TOTAL COLUMN 4: _____ (subtract from No. 2)
                    _____
(mark this number on horizontal line on the next page)

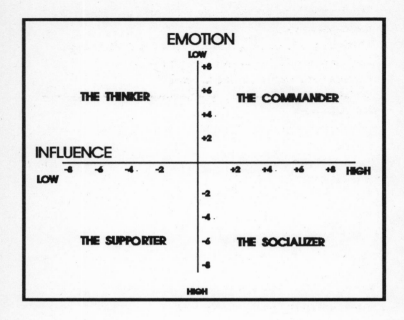

DEALING WITH THE DIFFERENT STYLES

IF YOU ARE A THINKER

Thinkers feel most at ease with you.

Thinkers prefer you continue at your slower pace and concentrate on details.

Commanders feel you probably should go somewhat faster.

Commanders prefer you to be more concerned with results than correctness.

Socializers feel you are far too detailed and far too careful.

Socializers prefer you to talk more and deal on a feelings level.

Supporters feel you confront too easily.

Supporters prefer if you would trust them more.

IF YOU ARE A COMMANDER

Thinkers feel you are too result orientated and may be intimidated by you.

Thinkers prefer dealing with you on a superficial range.

Commanders feel in competition with you.

Commanders prefer staying in control.

Socializers feel uneasy with you because they can't read you well enough.

Socializers prefer you withheld less information and weren't so pushy.

Supporters feel intimidated by you. You are far too result and task orientated for them.

Supporters prefer you developed some "people skills".

IF YOU ARE A SOCIALIZER

Thinkers feel you are nuts. They don't like your lack of concern for detail.

Thinkers prefer concrete plans. Chances are you prefer dreams and concepts.

Commanders feel you are too emotional and too talkative.

Commanders prefer staying in control and this causes conflict.

Socializers feel you are a long lost buddy.

Socializers prefer you let them talk more. They like your openness.

Supporters feel a lot like you but are not as aggressive.

Supporters prefer feelings to facts.

IF YOU ARE A SUPPORTER

Thinkers feel you are too emotional.

Thinkers prefer you too commit to more things.

Commanders feel you need more "guts" to go after things with more assertiveness.

Commanders prefer you deal with them on fact not feeling basis.

Socializers feel impatient toward you. You take too long to decide things.

Socializers prefer you give them the lead.
Supporters feel "warm fuzzies" around you.
Supporters prefer you to chat them up good before discussing the business at hand.

FLEXIBILITY IS THE KEY!

One of the greatest services we can offer to others is to provide an opportunity for them to be brought to wholeness. A place where people are loved, accepted and nourished. Life is tough. What people need, really need, cannot be found in a Sears catalogue.

Removing the Relational Success-Blockers, is not easy, in fact, it can cause conflict even in the best of relationships. Thus the next chapter, How to Handle Conflicts & Disagreements.

CHAPTER 10

HOW TO HANDLE CONFLICT & DISAGREEMENT

"We've lost that lovin' feeling, now it's gone,
gone, gone..."

So says a popular love song. How true! Even the best of relationships experience conflict and soon the lovin' feeling is gone. It happens between spouses, friends, co-workers, nations. Where people are, conflict will soon follow.

Conflict is common to relationships and may I say, normal. It can produce isolation or unity. It can kill or heal. It can be positive or negative. It can lead to greater understanding and strengthen relationships.

TELEVISION'S ROLE IN CONFLICT RESOLUTION

How has television taught us to resolve problems in the home? Think for a moment of each of these characters below and how they solve their interpersonal problems.

- Jackie Gleason on The Honeymooners
- Ozzie and Harriet on Father Knows Best
- The Cleaver's, Leave It To Beaver
- Archie Bunker on All In The Family
- The Keaton's on Family Ties
- The Cosby Show
- Rosanne
- Married with Children

CONFLICT DEFINED

A conflict is a clash between two wills. It can be called a disagreement or confrontation between two or more people. They are normal and necessary for growth provided they are faced and dealt with in effective ways.

Benefits of conflicts:

- Develops greater understanding.
- Greater awareness of each other's needs, wants and desires.
- Leads to meaningful dialogue.
- Develops you personally.

EXERCISE

Circle How You Feel Today.

Agree	Disagree	
1 2 3 4 5		I handle problems effectively
1 2 3 4 5		I am happy with the way I discuss problems
1 2 3 4 5		I am very good at conflict resolution
1 2 3 4 5		I allow others to express their opinion freely
1 2 3 4 5		I demonstrate my anger in appropriate ways
1 2 3 4 5		I can forgive others after disagreements
1 2 3 4 5		I do not avoid conflict
1 2 3 4 5		I have no outstanding interpersonal conflicts
1 2 3 4 5		I listen well to others during conflict
1 2 3 4 5		I focus on issues not people

CONFLICT TYPES

Conflict and disagreement problems generally fall into one of the following broad classifications or groupings.

1. The Big Mess

This occurs when many different unresolved situations have been lumped together. By this stage communication is poor or none existent. In this category the problems are identified by generalizing issues without necessarily stating the specific problems. "Jim and I have philosophical differences which have polarized the department."

2. The Performance Argument

In this case, people disagree about something more specific. This category concerns itself with expectations and roles. The problem is often stated as "Your problem is ..."

3. The "You Changed" Factor

Someone has changed the way of doing something, in this case. This deviation causes friction. If someone was a star performer and changes to a poor performer, conflict can occur.

4. The Stick in the Mud

This one is the opposite of the previous category. It says, "You don't want to change." This reluctance to move, shift or improve is a very prevalent source of conflict.

5. The Breakdown

This is probably the most common of all the conflict categories; the communication breakdown. It shows itself as either blow-ups, cooling of communications, messages being mixed-up, rubbing each other the wrong way all forcing a block to effective communication.

Think about some recent conflict you have faced in the past. Which category did it fall under? Here is another way of looking at what happens in conflict, in graphic form.

LEVELS OF COMMUNICATION

Effective communication in resolving conflict and disagreement requires communicating in more than superficial ways. This following scale may be helpful in depicting the different levels in the communicative process.

LEVEL 1. SUPERFICIAL

Superficial or Cliche communications allows a person to remain fairly safe and isolated. It is restricted to greetings and casual comments which deal mainly with data rather than opinion and feelings.

We are the least transparent on this level. We relate to the greatest number of people on this level.

LEVEL 2. DATA

Data communication is a discussion on factual level. It still holds people at arm's length.

LEVEL 3.   OPINION

Opinion communication involves the sharing and exchanging of ideas and personal opinions. This is the first stage of true communication. People are beginning to express what they feel.

LEVEL 4. GUT LEVEL

Gut level communication involves the sharing of emotion. It consists of sharing hopes, dreams, sorrows and joys. It gets to the feelings state of the people communicating. Real communication is exchanged on this level.

LEVEL 5. CORE

Core communication involves the complete emotional and personal truthfulness. Intimacy is transparent, sharing the real you. It is transferring the essence of your being. Very few of us ever get to this stage with many people. It involves deep personal disclosure.

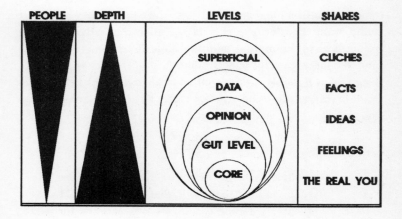

4 KEYS TO RESOLVE CONFLICT

> "YOU CAN'T SIMULTANEOUSLY PREVENT AND
> PREPARE FOR WAR."
>
> **Einstein**

KEY #1 LISTEN CAREFULLY

Resolving conflict requires a commitment to actively listen. Without effective listening, communication and corrective resolution is hopeless. How many times have you heard, "Pay attention, you're not listening to me".

LISTENING BLOCKERS

Distractions

One of the most common causes of poor listening is a tendency to become distracted. Let's face it, it's easy to let our mind wander. Because this is so, effective, active listening reminds us to eliminate as many possible distractions as possible and to concentrate sufficiently on the person we are supposed to listen to. If possible resolve conflict in an area which is free from walk-in interruptions or people walking by or the telephone ringing.

Details

How often has someone gone off on a tangent because of some detail that had little to do with what was being spoken. One barrier to effective listening can be an over concern for detail, missing the important and true issues.

Emotions

Certain people allow their emotions to block what is being said, thereby becoming poor listeners. Our emotions are powerful and need to be kept in check while listening lest we become carried away by feelings and not truly hear what is being said.

Faking

A real block to listening is what some people call "pseudo-listening". It is a form of pretending to be interested while being disinterested. When faking, you miss what is being said.

Protection

Protective listening is really selective listening. Either as a mechanism for protecting feelings or threatening messages or a sign of boredom, this barrier ruins the listening process. It only hears what it wants to hear. It can shut off anything too "deep or painful". Effective listening involves listening to the whole message.

Attitude

There are certain attitudes which demonstrate a listening interest and others which demonstrate lack of attention. Proper listening attitude conveys willingness to understand and accept. It shows itself by giving the message sender full attention. It allows for verification and clarification of meaning. It truly attempts to benefit by listening. It's an attitude that view's the other person as a valuable ally not an enemy.

LISTENING SKILLS

LISTEN FOR...	INSTEAD OF...
The meaning	The words
The message	The mode of delivery
Understanding	Prejudices
Solutions	Problems
Hurts	Targets of attack
Common Points	Divisive Issues

DO'S AND DON'TS FOR EFFECTIVE LISTENING

DO

- Give full attention
- Have an attitude of wanting to hear meanings
- Reflect back feelings and meanings
- Maintain eye contact
- Support what is being said with body gestures
- Control all possible distractions
- Summarize often what you think they are saying
- Provide feedback
- Ask questions if anything is unclear
- Match and mirror what they do with their body

DON'T

- Interrupt
- Fuss the details
- Manipulate the conversation
- Make assumptions

- Look away
- Put words in their mouth
- Make judgemental comments verbally or non-verbally
- Limit how "deep" they want to go
- Get off subject

KEY #2 CONFRONT CAREFULLY

Let's agree right now that if there are problems in relationships that go unresolved they will grow. If a relationship is to flourish it must deal with problems and conflict. We will examine two main issues relating to confrontation in conflict.

1. KEEPING THE FOCUS

A manager is concerned about a salesman who is constantly avoiding making the cold calls necessary to close sales to meet quota. He values the relationship enough to deal with conflict and is aware that at times it may mean confronting difficult situations.

The manager checks his attitude and motivation. "I care about this person. I value this salesman as a human being. I truly want to help not hurt." The manager chooses a location and a time which will make for effective communication and invites the salesman in to discuss the problem of cold calling. Rather than focusing on all aspects of sales, the manager shares that he would like to discuss one issue - cold calls. He describes the problem in specific terms and avoids judgemental calls that focus in on the individual. He states he wants to attack this issue not the individual. He shares facts, expresses his feelings and requests feedback from the agent, without interrupting allowing the salesman to share his views.

KEEP THE FOCUS...

ON...	INSTEAD OF...
Me	You
One concern	Many issues
The problem	The person
Behaviour	Personality
Specifics	Generalizations
Meaning	Hidden meanings
Facts	Assumptions

2. USE AN APPROPRIATE STYLE (NOT ONLY YOUR DOMINANT STYLE) TO RESOLVE CONFLICT.

If two partners in business have a conflict they will resolve one of five ways. The same applies for a teenager and his father or a girlfriend and her boyfriend or a wife and her husband. It applies everywhere conflict exist.

The two factors which govern which method someone chooses to resolve conflict are 1) How much they value the relationship, 2) How much they value the goal; that is, the issue causing the disagreement. People can rate themselves as either High or Low on each line.

People who value the relationship highly but not the goal, resolve conflict by YIELDING. They really dislike conflict and would prefer to not push for their side of the issue so they just give in. People who neither value the goal or are not as concerned with the relationship WITHDRAW. Because an issue is not important in their minds and they don't care if the relationship is maintained they tend to resolve issues by mentally or physically packing it in. Not an effective way of building long-tern, solid relationships.

People who don't care much about maintaining the relationship but very much want to achieve the goal solve relationship problems by trying to WIN. What is really important to these people is to do whatever they want to do.

Since they are more concerned with getting their way as opposed to relational harmony they go for results not relationships.

Most people think COMPROMISE is the best way to deal with conflict. I disagree. I think it is better than some of the others but it has some downfalls as well. Compromise says that I somewhat value the relationship and I somewhat value the goal. Well what do you do if you strongly value the goal?

The most productive method of resolving conflict is to RESOLVE it. Notice that this method rates the relationship really high and rates the goal really high as well.

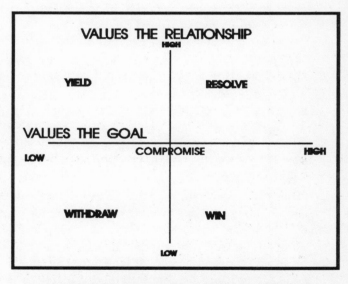

CONFLICT RESOLUTION STYLES

KEY #3 FORGIVE WILLINGLY

Strains in marriages, friendships, business relationships, national harmony can cause isolation and division. In fact,
as the following chart illustrates, Wars begin with Spats.

BEHAVIOUR	CLASSIFICATION	RESULT
Difference of Opinion	Spat	Confrontation
Heated Argument	Quarrel	Division
Intense Anger	Fight	Rejection
Hostility	War	Separation

WARS BEGIN WITH SPATS

The fastest way to resolve conflict is to seek forgiveness
when wrong, and freely forgive when wronged. It let's the steam
out of the pressure cooker of resentment and anger. Forgiveness
should be expressed verbally and specifically. This is a difficult
request but the effect of the forgiveness will be enhanced if this
step is followed. True forgiveness also avoids conditions. It's not,
"I'll forgive if... or I'll forgive you but..." Remember forgiveness
builds harmony and diffuses conflict.

How many people do you know go to their grave bitter
and resentful, hating someone they refused to forgive for years?
Or someone losing a loved one before they had a chance to repair
a strained relationship. By the way, if that has happened to you,
I hope you please forgive yourself. If your father or mother or
friend passed away before you could tell them you were sorry or
that you forgive them or just how much you really loved them,
please forgive yourself. Don't carry that around any longer. Let
go!

KEY #4 ACT DECISIVELY

Like any other significant or worthwhile thing in life, action is required. The same is true in relationships. Resolution of conflict requires a willingness to decide to act. John Clyde, a leading management consultant offers four specific statements or questions people can ask in conflict situations.

IF I HAVE A PROBLEM WITH YOU, I COULD SAY...

"I HAVE A PROBLEM AND I NEED YOUR HELP. ARE YOU WILLING TO HELP?"

"WHEN YOU DO THIS..." (LIST SPECIFICALLY WHAT THEY DO WHICH CAUSES YOU CONCERN.)

"I FEEL..."

"WHAT CAN I DO?"

CONFLICT WORKSHEET

Instructions: When faced with a conflict or a disagreement which interferes with the relationship, deal with it by both parties completing this worksheet. It will help identify and solve the problem.

MY CONCERN: As I see it, the problem is...

YOUR CONCERN: As far as I can see, you feel...

SOLUTION: The best way to deal with this is...

FORGIVENESS: The attitude I should have now is...

ACTION: Specifically, perhaps we should...

CONCLUSION

The lovely Dallas broadcaster, Suzie Humphreys said, "The greatest lessons I've ever had to learn came in some form of devastation." The same is true of me. "If God was going to give you some great lesson in life, would He wrap it up in fancy paper put a big bow on it and serve it to you on a silver platter?" asked Dr. Norman Vincent Peale. No, of course not!

My passion, which I have attempted to articulate in these pages is to convey hope even in the midst of adversity. For many readers, life may find them at a happy and successful juncture. I congratulate them but remind them to prepare for times when it may not be so. Life will test you deeply. If you have as yet been untested, trials will be inevitable. Frustration and heartbreak are to pass your way at some time. It does so for all of us. So enjoy the present but prepare for the future.

For other readers, life is far from "sunshine and roses". I want to remind you that challenges and obstacles do go away. Your Berlin wall will come crumbling down. After the rain does (eventually) come the sunshine. See obstacles as a chance to grow and learn. It's what happens "in" us that matters, not what happens "to" us. Agree to conquer your obstacles no matter what. Be committed to winning! You see, in life there are no obstacles only a shortage of ideas.

Never give up, never give in. Hold onto your dreams and goals even if you don't have the whole solution to seeing those dreams turn into realities. Never throw ideals away because you don't have the whole picture or because it might fail. Every great idea has some failure factors. So what if something fails, big deal. Will you be richer for it? You bet!

Does conquering your obstacles seem impossible? Then for you, it is impossible. Change your mind. Conquer your obstacles. You have what it takes plus there are other resources to help along the way. Seek out the answers.

The very last thing my father said to me before he died was "You made it." My dad didn't think I would make it to his bedside in time because I was in prison, serving a sentence for armed robbery. Seven months later, the very last thing my older brother Ivan told me before he died was "Take care of yourself." I can't tell them today but if I could, I would say "I'm making it!" and "I am taking care of myself." And to you, I say "You are going to make it! Take care of yourself".

Gerry Robert

CONQUERING LIFE'S OBSTACLES

Couldn't someone that you know benefit from reading CONQUERING LIFE'S OBSTACLES? It is the perfect gift for anyone looking to enjoy more happiness, health and wealth.

Please rush me _____ copies at $16.95 each, including shipping. Add 7% GST . I have enclosed a cheque made payable to Prime Performance Corporation in the amount of $_____. Charge my credit card:

☐ Visa ☐ MasterCard ☐ American Express

Account Number

Signature_____Expiry Date_____

Full Name:_____

Address:_____

City:_____Prov._____

Postal Code:_____Telephone:_____

For an order of ten or more books we offer a discount. Please write us for details, or call us at (416) 886-9252, FAX: (416) 886-0126.
PRIME PERFORMANCE CORPORATION, (PPC Books),
42 Niles Way, Thornhill, Ontario, Canada, L3T 5B8

CONQUERING LIFE'S OBSTACLES

Couldn't someone that you know benefit from reading <u>CONQUERING LIFE'S OBSTACLES</u>? It is the perfect gift for anyone looking to enjoy more happiness, health and wealth.

Please rush me _____ copies at $16.95 each, including shipping. Add 7% GST . I have enclosed a cheque made payable to Prime Performance Corporation in the amount of $_____. Charge my credit card:

☐ Visa   ☐ MasterCard   ☐ American Express

Account Number

Signature_____Expiry Date_____

Full Name:_____

Address:_____

City:_____Prov._____

Postal Code:_____Telephone:_____

For an order of ten or more books we offer a discount. Please write us for details, or call us at (416) 886-9252, FAX: (416) 886-0126.
PRIME PERFORMANCE CORPORATION, (PPC Books),
42 Niles Way, Thornhill, Ontario, Canada, L3T 5B8